SCHADENFREUDE

SCHADENFREUDE

A Handy Guide to the Glee Found in Others' Misery

Lawrence Dorfman

In collaboration with James Michael Naccarato

Skyhorse Publishing

Skyhorse Publishing books may be purchased in bulk at special discounts for sales promotion, corporate gifts, fund-raising, or educational purposes. Special editions can also be created to specifications. For details, contact the Special Sales Department, Skyhorse Publishing, 307 West 36th Street, 11th Floor, New York, NY 10018 or info@skyhorse-publishing.com.

Skyhorse® and Skyhorse Publishing® are registered trademarks of Skyhorse Publishing, Inc.®, a Delaware corporation.

Visit our website at www.skyhorsepublishing.com.

10 9 8 7 6 5 4 3 2 1

Library of Congress Cataloging-in-Publication Data is available on file.

ISBN: 978-1-62636-174-4

Printed in China

To the Three Stooges, the Marx Brothers, Abbott
and Costello, Soupy Sales, Charlie Chaplin, Buster Keaton,
Harold Lloyd, Laurel and Hardy, and most of all,
Bugs Bunny and the WB gang.

Schadenfreude personified.

TABLE OF CONTENTS

INTRODUCTION

Lisa: Dad, do you know what Schadenfreude is?

Homer: No, I don't know what "shaden-frawde" is. Please tell me, because I'm dying to know.

Lisa: It's a German term for "shameful joy," taking pleasure in the suffering of others.

Homer: Oh, come on, Lisa. I'm just glad to see him fall flat on his butt! He's usually all happy and comfortable, and surrounded by loved ones, and it makes me feel . . . What's the opposite of that shameful joy thing of yours?

Lisa: Sour grapes.

Homer: Boy, those Germans have a word for everything!
                                                        —*The Simpsons*

The origins of "One man's pain is another man's pleasure" can be found in old English texts circa mid-1500s, and has been used in a variety of ways since ("one man's meat is another man's poison," etc.).

There are two kinds of Schadenfreude:
In the early part of the nineteenth century until today, the physical aspects of Schadenfreude could be seen in the broadness of slapstick comedy—from the base humor of someone slipping on a banana peel, to getting hit in the face or head with a 2 x 4, to falling off a ladder, to stepping on a rake, all the way up to the seemingly endless stream of getting kicked/punched/rammed in the genitals that made up the bulk of the entertainment that was *America's Funniest Home Videos* and *Jackass*. Their pain is palpable and, to many watching, riotously funny.

The other kind manifested itself in a slightly more cerebral way . . . the joy one takes when someone lets their success go to their head and, as a result, becomes an obnoxious bore. It is the pleasure we take on seeing who gets fired on *The Apprentice* or who gets voted off the island on *Survivor*. When they eventually screw up (and they do, more often than not), there is a feeling that overtakes us that can only be described with that very German word: Schadenfreude.

These days, those "downfalls" are the main source of most news reporting, whether on television, radio, via Twitter and Facebook, and in pretty much all media. There is nothing that sells papers or attracts viewers like a good scandal involving a celebrity, a politician, or a sports star who has been caught breaking the rules.

Picture this . . .

You're walking down the street in, say, New York City, and you spy a man knocking a woman and her small child out of the way as they try to catch a cab. The man, an upstanding lion of business, is in a hurry and his business meeting (or whatever) is going to take precedent over the mere needs of a mom and her offspring. The cab pulls out and gets hit broadside by another cab. No one is hurt . . . but that elation you feel, knowing that the guy in the cab is going to miss his "important" meeting . . . why, that's SCHADENFREUDE.

SCHADENFREUDE comes in many shapes and colors. It can be as simple as cheering and clapping that follows a waitress dropping a tray of dishes or a bartender breaking a glass.

It can be the exultant gladness one feels when a stunningly beautiful contestant in a major beauty contest gives an answer to a question that clearly shows her to have the IQ of a Q-tip.

It can be the unexpected pleasure one feels while watching a young actor or actress, who has not done *any* work of significance in his/her short and not particularly stellar career, get arrested for drugs . . . or bad driving . . . or shoplifting . . . or any myriad of possible infractions that you know will have major consequences down the road. And the immediate image that pops into your head where they're wearing an orange jersey while they spear trash on the side of the road under the supervision of an armed guard . . . that's SCHADENFREUDE.

Admit it . . . it forms the basis of much of our humor. From the slapstick of the *3 Stooges* to the *Keystone Cops* to Charlie Chaplin, Buster Keaton, and Harold Lloyd . . . on through Chevy Chase's pratfalls at the beginning of the early days of *Saturday Night Live* . . . to the angst of *The Hangover* and pretty much every Steve Carell movie . . . we laugh instinctively at the misfortunes of others . . . and if the recipients have been presented as vicious or evil or arrogant or condescending . . . well, there is a level of satisfaction that comes from seeing revenge enacted. That feeling of satisfaction from a perceived justice? That's SCHADENFREUDE.

This book contains all sorts of examples, miniature portraits of characters from all walks of life who rose to the pinnacle of their various fields... often on the backs of others . . . committed all levels of atrocities while up there . . . and ultimately fell from grace . . . a hard, damaging, brutal fall (oft times fatal) and the sense of satisfaction that was felt as a result . . . yep, you guessed it . . . SCHADENFREUDE.

CHAPTER ONE

HISTORY

"History teaches us that men and nations behave wisely once they have exhausted all other alternatives."

—Abba Eban

We fill history with good guys and bad guys—too bad they're usually the same person. It just depends on who's telling their stories. General Custer and Wyatt Earp had devoted wives who knitted heroic stories of their husbands instead of booties. Benedict Arnold and Richard Nixon . . . not so much. It wasn't that long ago that Americans cheered moving the Indians (or Redskins as they were then known) out of their way and off to the reservation. Today, we've ceded millions of dollars in gambling revenue to atone for our guilt over the tragic displacement of Native Americans. The only truth is what we want it to be, or, as Winston Churchill said, "History will be kind to me for I intend to write it." Read quickly my friends for yesterday's joker is certain to become tomorrow's Batman.

History is rife with Schadenfreude. From the giggling that started amongst the other animals in the garden while the snake sold Adam and Eve a bill of goods, to the French peasants eating pound cake while Marie Antoinette lost her head, to Abbie Hoffman sitting in front of his television eating a bowl of ice cream and chortling while Nixon flashed the Peace sign as he boarded that last plane, to watching a "secret" video that ends up swaying an election, Schadenfreude has been a constant emotion that has enveloped many of the participants.

ALEXANDER THE GREAT

Perhaps the greatest general of all times, Alexander set his sights on creating the largest empire the world had ever seen. Apparently, thinking he was going to live forever, he paid little mind to the fact that most empires are built on successive generations. So when gravely ill and asked to name an heir, Alexander ignored his son and his trusted officers and simply replied, "the strongest." Gee, you think? It comes as no surprise that as a result of this lack of endorsement, his empire would experience nearly 200 years of war and end up destroying just about everything he had tried to accomplish.

JULIUS CAESAR

Julius Caesar was a Roman general, a statesman, and an author. He also triggered the beginning of the end of the Roman Empire. Power hungry from the jump, he pissed off the Senate and practically everyone in it. He refused to give up his military command and started a civil war as a result. No one was happy . . . and so he was assassinated in the very same Senate by his cronies, led by his friend Brutus.

There is some controversy over whether he actually uttered the infamous line, "Et tu, Brute?" Latin for "And you, Brutus?" Other than the fact that they spoke Greek at the time, no one knows. I prefer to think . . . yes, after having subjected his friends to all manner of embarrassment.

"Et tu, Brute?" You bet your ass, Julie.

PAUL OF TARSUS

So we got this guy named Saul living in the city of Tarsus around 20 AD. He's a Jew and boy does he hate these up- and-coming Christians. Any chance he gets he persecutes them. We don't know exactly what that means, but we assume it's more than taking their lunch money or setting fire to bags of shit outside their stable doors. He's happy, just kicking back, trading stories of what they did to this Christian or what they did to this one; you know, the one who already looks like a mosaic. Life could not be finer. Until one night on the road to Damascus he has a vision and it's a whopper. He sees the risen Jesus who asks him, "Why are you persecuting me?" Either because he was a smart-aleck or maybe because he was just buying time, Saul has the nerve to ask, "Who are you?" Remember: he's talking to a vision that none of his companions can see. "I am Jesus, the one you are per-secuting." Not the answer he was expecting. Jesus then sends him back to the city, making him temporarily blind, just so his mind doesn't wander. After three days his vision returns and Saul, now called Paul, becomes a pillar of the Church, which in those days usually meant an extremely painful death.

TOWER OF PISA

Construction of this Italian bell tower occurred in three stages across 344 years. Don't you think that someone might have noticed at some point that the ground was too unstable to support a 186-foot tower that weighs 14,500 metric tons? In what is surely the finest example of "not my job," work continued, even though the tower began to lean less than ten years after construction began. Yep, they continued to build for another 334 YEARS! They even had to compensate by adding additional steps on the south-facing staircase, meaning that the top of the tower is displaced by over 12 feet from where it would be if it was straight.

The English feel schaden-freude even about themselves.

—Martin Amis

RICHARD III

As Lord Protector, Richard, Duke of York (the future Richard III), was appointed to take care of his nephews, the two young sons of King Edward IV, after the latter's sudden death. Can you say wolf guarding the hen house? Soon the princes are "lodged" in the Tower of London. (Like having the penthouse suite at Alcatraz.) Well, you know the trouble kids can get into. Seems that they disappeared . . . forever. And who benefited from the disappearances—well, Uncle Dick, who was soon crowned king.

CHRISTOPHER COLUMBUS

Despite popular mythology, it was widely accepted at the time of Columbus that the world was round. There was even a fairly accurate estimate of how big it was. Chris had researched all this, but apparently, had been absent from class when one small little detail had been discussed. It seems that most of the estimates came from Muslim scholars and their "mile" was longer than the European "mile." Columbus never made the conversion and was convinced that the world was only 15,000 miles in diameter. That would make his trek to the riches of the Orient just slightly longer than going out for milk. You can imagine how angry his crew must have been—especially after the fourth ship fell over the edge.

BENEDICT ARNOLD

Benedict Arnold was a distinguished Continental Army officer during the early days of the American Revolution. It was Arnold who suggested that the colonial troops attack the poorly-defended Fort Ticonderoga. That plan promoted him to colonel in the Connecticut militia. His expedition to attack Quebec through the Maine wilderness would ultimately earn him the rank of Brigadier General in the Continental Army. Although not without a few setbacks, Arnold's career among the patriots continued to grow and he became the military commander of Philadelphia, which

allowed him a lavish lifestyle. It was there that he met and soon married Peggy Shippen, and in the words of 10cc, the "things we do for love." Peggy, who came from a loyalist family, had been courted by British Major John Andre and she remained in touch with him. Taking advantage of Arnold's opinion of the deplorable conditions in the former colonies, the Brits began to tap him for information. Soon wife Peggy was sending Andre letters encoded with secret messages from her husband. It all began to unravel when Andre was captured. Benedict Arnold, early hero of the revolution, was at last exposed as a traitor to the new country.

MARIE ANTOINETTE

Perhaps best remembered as the world's greatest caterer ("let them eat cake"), Marie

Antoinette should have been the first to ask Pat Sajak to buy a clue. Instead, she blissfully went about her business while Paris ran red in blood. Imprisoned by the French Revolution, she lost her crown, her mind and . . . her head. Ouch.

NAPOLEON BONAPARTE

In 1812, Napoleon was lured deep into Russia, where the undefeated French emperor led a force of 500,000 soldiers into Moscow, which he found abandoned and burning. At this point, Mr. Bonaparte would be the first to quote Emily Litella and mumble, "Never Mind." He turned his troops around and began what is affectionately called "The Great Retreat." By the time he crossed the Berezina River, nearly 380,000 men were dead and 100,000 more cap-

tured by the Russians. It was about then that he began what we like to call the "Great Save My Ass," abandoning his troops and fleeing to Paris. Eventually, he would be found out and after being exiled a couple of times, he would die in his bed, his hand, no doubt, wedged beneath his jammies.

JOHN WILKES BOOTH

Someone explain this to me. A third-rate actor, living in his brother's shadow, gathers together a group of conspirators who plan to do what the whole of the Southern states could not do—bring about the collapse of the Union. And they nearly

accomplish it. I don't know what is harder to believe—Booth's hubris or how easy it was for his plan to work. I get that he was a familiar face at the Ford's Theatre but still, how was he able to slip into the President's box and shoot him? Clearly he had no escape plan—he jumped on stage and, in the process, injured his leg. Despite this, how was he still able to escape the theatre, which was less than two miles from the White House? It's wartime in Washington, DC. Where were all the soldiers? Co-conspirator Lewis Powell was able to get to Secretary of State William H. Seward in his home and stab him. Then it took three days to find Powell and another eleven to track down Booth and kill him. Now remember—the greatest military minds in the South had succeeded in waging a war for independence that had lasted four years and was not going well. A group of misfits who could barely get out of their own way nearly accomplished the same thing in a night out at the theatre.

GENERAL GEORGE CUSTER

After graduating dead last in his West Point class, General George Custer thought that it would make sense to mount a frontal attack with 200 men against 2,000 Sioux and Cheyenne warriors. Outnumbered 10-to-1, he then had another great idea—let's not wait for reinforcements. It still causes historians to scratch their heads. Some of them believe that this suicidal stand at Little Big Horn was fueled by Custer's ambition to become president. Whatever his reasoning, by sundown that bloated ambition had been deflated by a hail of arrows. As if that wasn't bad enough, over the years, portraying this nutjob as a heroic figure has challenged a truly sad of actors, including Marcello Mastroianni, Richard Mulligan, Leslie Nielsen, and Ronald Reagan. The pain never ends.

WESTERN UNION

In 1876, a Western Union internal memo stated, "This 'telephone' has too many shortcomings to be seriously considered as a means of communication. The device is inherently of no value to us." Comfortable with the monopoly they had on the telegraph system, they turned down the patent for Alexander Graham Bell's new invention. Bell had offered it to them for $100,000: two years later, they would try to buy it for $25 million. It might be the first time anyone ever got a busy signal.

ULYSSES S. GRANT

Ulysses S. Grant was a celebrated war general of the Civil War who led the North to victory. Unfortunately, he was less celebrated as the 18th President of the United States. The future resident of Grant's Tomb faced eleven scandals in his two terms. Corrupt appointees were accused of fraud in the Treasury department, the Post Office, the Patent Office, Secretary of Navy and other posts. The question remains—did the corruption occur because he was a drunk, or did the scandals cause him to drink? In any event, this led G. K. Chesterton to quote, "It is enough to add that he was a very good general and a very bad president."

WILLIAM GLADSTONE

Gladstone was a British statesman who served as Prime Minister of Great Britain four times. His many "accomplishments" include his role in the disestablishment of the Church of Ireland and the introduction of secret voting. He loved power and was known for entering into rivalries with many of the leaders of the day, most famously Benjamin Disraeli. He was also known as the "G.O.M." (Grand Old Man), although Disraeli changed that to "God's Only Mistake."

AMBROSE BIERCE

Bierce was an American journalist who wrote for the San Francisco Examiner in the late 1800s. Celebrated for his biting social commentary and satire, he wrote ghost and war stories, but is best known for his collection of snarky definitions entitled *The Devil's Dictionary.* Suffering from an acute condition of self-importance, at age seventy-one he joined Pancho Villa's army to gain a firsthand look at the Mexican Revolution, and quickly vanished without a trace. Sadly, he had predicted his own demise in his cynical definition of a non-combatant, which he defined as being a "dead Quaker."

It is impossible to suffer without making someone pay for it; every complaint already contains revenge.
—**Friedrich Nietzsche**

TITANIC

The RMS Titanic was the largest passenger steamship in the world and was popularly believed to be unsinkable. Unfortunately, no one told that to the iceberg. Add to that the fact that there was an inadequate supply of lifeboats, design flaws that included an unreliable system of watertight compartments and poor-quality rivets in the ship's hull, and what do you get—a $2 billion-grossing film that won eleven Academy Awards and still pisses me off every time I think of Rose throwing that necklace into the ocean over the wreck site. I mean, what, there wasn't a single family member who could have used it?

PROHIBITION

Who could have possibly thought this was a good idea?

In 1920, the 18th Amendment was put into effect banning the sale, production, and transportation of alcohol. Killer booze was going to be a thing of the past. Decent God-fearing women could keep their weak husbands home at night, and all roads would be paved with gold. Yeah, not so much. The prohibition of alcohol lit a fire under organized crime that made hell look like a Bic lighter. And because we know how well criminals get along, this resulted in truly spectacular gangland violence. (St. Valentine's Day Massacre, anyone?) Distilleries and breweries across our borders flourished, and booze slipped in, while almost every border agent and cop discovered that Christmas was now coming year round. Al Capone, Bugs Moran, and a myriad of others ran very lucrative bootlegging operations and speakeasies. The mob became entrenched into the very fabric of American culture. All because a few blue hairs didn't want to drink. Oh, and after booze was made illegal, the government needed to find a way to raise money to compensate for all that lost alcohol tax; so they came up with the federal income tax. Now I need a drink.

Adolf Hitler

Imagine how much better off the world would have been if he could only be remembered as a bad painter. "I have a *Dogs Playing Poker, A Velvet Elvis* on velvet, and an A. Hitler." Tell you what, you can have all three for 100 bucks. But it's got to be cash.

Benito Mussolini

After ruling Italy poorly from 1922 to 1943, Mussolini was executed by communist partisans. Was that good enough for the Italians? Not a chance. His body was dumped in a Piazza in Milan, where it was kicked, spat upon, and hung upside down for all the world to see from the roof of an Esso gas station. But he did get the trains to run on time.

George Patton

A brilliant general during WWII, Patton led his troops through occupied France and, ultimately, right into Nazi Germany at the end of the war. But as Paul Harvey was fond of saying, "Now here's the rest of the story." Patton was a bonafide bastard and Eisenhower didn't trust him as far as he could throw him. After two high-profile incidents where he slapped and verbally abused soldiers hospitalized with battle fatigue (PTSD today), Eisenhower reprimanded him and kept him from command for nearly a year. Patton was a racist, compared the Nazis to Democrats and Republicans, and once suggested that his soldiers could "drive the British back into the sea." A strong believer in reincarnation, Patton sought nobility, convinced that he had been a reincarnated soldier who had fought in prehistoric times. He also thought he was a Greek soldier fighting the Persians, an infantryman under Napoleon, and a legionnaire with Julius Caesar. Fat chance—he was more likely the bully who had frequently tasted the business end of the switch. Totally out of touch with the consequences of his actions, he bragged that he'd had a long-term affair with his niece, who was the same age as his daughters, and who called him

"Uncle Georgie." The girl would commit suicide when confronted about the affair. Patton would die as a result of injuries sustained in a car crash. He spent the last days of his life paralyzed from the neck down, knowing that if he survived, he would never resume a normal life. George C. Scott notwithstanding, Patton certainly got what he deserved.

AMELIA EARHART

Amelia Earhart was an aviation pioneer. She set a number of flying records, including being the first female pilot to fly solo across the Atlantic Ocean. She wrote bestselling books and is often cited as an inspiration for women's independence and, specifically, learning to fly. Hello? She got lost. Never came back. I don't know about you, but if I'm going to feel inspired, I want it to come from someone who accomplished what they set out to do. I'd even settle for someone who failed but who can give me pointers on what to avoid. "So, Amelia, what do you think got you where you are today? Amelia? Hello, Amelia? Testing . . . one . . . two. Amelia?"

NEVILLE CHAMBERLAIN

Perhaps one of the first to actually have been interested in buying the Brooklyn Bridge, gullible, thy name was Chamberlain. Early in his position as prime minister, Neville Chamberlain looked for ways to placate Germany. His objective was to enlist Germany as a partner in creating a stable Europe. Never mind that the rest of the world was beginning to look at Hitler and his faithful Italian friend, Mussolini, as a "Danger, Will Robinson!" situation. Ignoring all that, Chamberlain flew to Germany and had a series of meetings with the big man himself where, bowing to the extortion by the Nazis, he allowed Germany to "annex" Austria. Then he tried to convince Czechoslovakia to surrender a chunk of their land to ensure "peace in our time." Yeah, right. He also persuaded Hitler to sign the Anglo–German Agreement, which basically said that England and Germany would never go to war again. He was one tough negotiator. Smug in his accomplishments, it would take him years to realize how wrong he had been about practically everything. He resigned from office and died in 1940 before the magnitude of the Nazi atrocities came to light.

ALBERT EINSTEIN

He developed the general theory of relativity, created the world's most famous equation

(E=mc^2), and was instrumental in establishing quantum theory. He published over 300 scientific papers, and his achievements made the name "Einstein" synonymous with genius. But he did so poorly in school and had such odd habits that his parents thought he was mentally retarded.

CHE GUEVARA

Ernesto "Che" Guevara was an Argentine Marxist revolutionary, physician, author, guerrilla leader, diplomat, and military theorist. A major figure of the Cuban Revolution, Che became a hero to a generation of revolutionaries (not to mention self-indulged college students). While carrying on the people's war in Bolivia, Che was betrayed by a Cuban exile-turned-CIA operative and captured by Bolivian Special Forces. Then, just to make sure he was given that final noble exit, a thirty-one-year-old alcoholic army sergeant is assigned as his executioner. Nine bullets later—five of which struck his legs—Che was dead. They had succeeded in killing the man, but they had inadvertently given birth to a t-shirt legacy that remains to this very day.

WINSTON CHURCHILL

Regarded as one of the all-time great wartime leaders of the twentieth century, Winston Churchill was born into a family with a history of mental illness. His father exhibited psychotic behaviors his entire life. His sister, Diana, would commit suicide following years of depression. Churchill dealt with his own reoccurring bouts of depression, which he called the "black dog." There are some who believe his depression helped him to realistically evaluate the threat of Hitler. Excuse me? Do you mean to tell me that having a chronically-depressed leader during a war which ended with the detonation of an atomic bomb, is somehow a good thing? But, then again, mental illness seems to be the prerequisite of being a world leader these days. Churchill was just ahead of his time.

Revenge is often like biting a dog because the dog bit you.
　　　　—**Austin O'Malley**

styling and specifications were the result of very sophisticated market analysis. This "e" car (for experimental) emerged from a development effort that would essentially guarantee its broad acceptance by the buying public when it was introduced. Boy, were they wrong. The Edsel—as it was to be called and as it will live on in infamy—never gained popularity, and Ford lost millions . . . and comedians everywhere had a new Tausman.

EDSEL

In the early 1950s, the Ford Motor Company came up with a new strategy to compete with General Motors and Chrysler, and increase their share of the domestic automobile market. They would build a car that would surpass all others. They assured their investors, and the Detroit automotive press, that this car's

BAY OF PIGS

Ticked off at Castro's control of Cuba (and the loss of all the cash that had been flowing freely into US businesses *and* mobsters), JFK approved a plan to invade and wrestle the country back into corruption . . . I mean freedom. A group of anti-Castro exiles were secretly trained and funded by the CIA. Well, not so secret—

both Cuba and their Soviet allies knew all about it days in advance. Roughly 1,400 quasi-soldiers set out from Guatemala by boat on April 17, 1961. CIA-supplied bombers began attacking Cuban airfields. It was all going according to plan. Problem was, the plan sucked. Within three days, they were defeated by Castro's forces. This was a major embarrassment for the new Kennedy Administration, and a big win for Castro, who would go on to lead his country for almost fifty more years. Castro henchman Che Guevara actually sent a note to Kennedy thanking him for the Bay of Pigs Invasion. "Before the attack, the revolution was weak. Now it is stronger than ever." Rub it in, why don't you? Kennedy lit a Cuban cigar.

CHERNOBYL

On April 26, 1986, top Soviet nuclear scientists were per-forming an experiment to test a new emergency core cooling feature at the Chernobyl Nuclear Power Plant in the Ukraine. Oops! The catastrophic power increase that resulted caused an explosion at the reactor core, which dispersed large quantities of radioactive fuel and core materials into the atmosphere, in what is considered the worst nuclear power plant accident in history. But no one ever needed to purchase a light bulb again.

EXXON VALDEZ

The Exxon Valdez oil tanker was traveling through the Prince William Sound in Alaska on its way to Long Beach, California, carrying about 55 million gallons of crude oil. But not for long. With the captain in his bunk sleeping off a bender, the third mate was at the helm. Everything would have gone smoothly if he had only looked at his radars, or, more accurately, turned it on! Instead, the Valdez struck Bligh Reef and spilled nearly 750,000 barrels of oil covering 1,300 miles of coastline and 11,000 square miles of ocean. One of the most devastating human-caused environmental disasters of all time, with as many as 250,000 seabirds, 2,800 sea otters, 300 harbor seals, 247 Bald Eagles, and 22 orcas killed. Not to mention the fifth of Wild Turkey that kept the experienced officer from the bridge.

THE WEATHERMEN

The Weathermen were a group of egocentric extreme left-wing radicals, who showered America with terrorism to prove how bad the government was. Allegedly taking the name from the Bob Dylan lyric, "You don't need a weatherman to know which way the wind blows," it seems more apt due to just how often they got things wrong. They set off bombs, incited riots, even helped Timothy Leary escape from prison . . . and nothing changed. In the end, most of what they accomplished would be confined to the misery they inflicted on their own—three killed while making bombs in NY, with countless others forced to live lies as they hid their new identities from loved ones, afraid that with every knock on the door their world would come crashing down. As Dylan would warn in the same song, "Better jump down a man-hole, light yourself a candle." 'Cause they still have a cell with your name on it.

During World War I, German General Erich Ludendorff observed, "The English fight like lions." Yes, a staff officer replied, "but they are led by donkeys." So, let's enjoy the fitting demise of a drove of donkeys.

CHAPTER TWO

RELIGION

"To judge from the notions expounded by theologians, one must conclude that God created most men simply with a view to crowding hell."

—Marquis de Sade

Killer Popes. Pedophile priests. Vicious Vicars. Audacious Abbots. Ruinous Rabbis. . . . You name it and there is that moment every year since time immemorial when one of those "pious" men has fallen from up high, subjected himself (since they are mostly men) to ridicule, and evoked a Schadenfreude amongst a following that rivals no other.

WORLD CHURCH OF
THE CREATOR

World Church of the Creator, or as it is known today, The Creativity Movement, is a white separatist organization that advocates a whites-only religion, Creativity. Founded in 1973 by Ben Klassen, it is an atheistic movement, with the term "creator" referring not to a deity, but to its members—its all-white members. It has been classified as a Neo-Nazi organization. Ya think? It's about as religious as a bake sale. After Klassen's suicide in 1993 (the religion, as well as the rest of us, believes suicide for its members is okay), Creativity almost died out as a religion until the new Church of the Creator was established three years later by Matthew F. Hale. These hate groups pop up like weeds. The good thing is that they are stoopid weeds. In 2005, Hale was sentenced to forty years in prison for soliciting an undercover FBI informant to kill a federal judge.

Envy is one of the seven deadly sins. Schadenfreude is very different in that it can keep you out of the confessional.

—Anonymous

THE CHURCH OF ALL
WORLDS

The Church of All Worlds is a neo-pagan religion founded in 1962 by Oberon Zell-Ravenheart and his wife, Morning Glory Zell-Ravenheart. Okay, that should be enough right there, but it gets better. The inspiration for this spiritual circle jerk is the science fiction novel, *Stranger in a Strange Land,* by Robert A. Heinlein. Yep, a piece of fiction. It's sometimes hard enough not to look at ALL religion as pieces of fiction, but most don't come with a copyright date. Zell-Ravenheart recently founded The Grey School of Wizardry, inspired in part by Hogwarts School of Witchcraft and Wizardry, the school in the Harry Potter novels. Can't wait to see what *50 Shades* brings.

THE CHURCH OF EUTHANASIA (CoE)

The Church of Euthanasia (CoE) is a political organization started by the Reverend Chris Korda in Boston, Massachusetts. It is "a non-profit educational foundation devoted to restoring balance between Humans and the remaining species on Earth." And how do we do that? We follow the Church's one commandment: "Thou shalt not procreate." The CoE also has four prin-

cipal pillars: suicide, abortion, cannibalism ("strictly limited to consumption of the already-dead"), and sodomy ("any sexual act not intended for procreation"). Slogans employed by the group include "Save the Planet, Kill Yourself," "Six Billion Humans Can't Be Wrong," and "Eat a Queer Fetus for Jesus."

He who has not the spirit of this age, has all the misery of it.
—Voltaire

JOAN OF ARC

So, I'm a twelve-year-old peasant girl in rural France and I start having hallucinations. I see Saint Michael, Saint Catherine and Saint Margaret. They all say the same thing—drive out the English and bring Charles VII to the throne. Remember: they're saying that to a twelve-year-old. Just because they're saints with visions doesn't mean that they know what they're doing. Well, Joan turns out to be an expert military strategist, and she leads the French to a series of victories which reverses the tide of the war. As George W. Bush would later say, "Mission Accomplished." But Joan continues to fight as one truce after another is signed then broken. Inevitably, she finds herself a captive of the English. Abandoned by the French and their shifting politics, Joan is convicted of heresy and burned at the stake—three times—just to make sure. Saint Michael, Saint Catherine and Saint Margaret were suspiciously quiet except for a brief "oops" that was heard amidst the snap, crackle and pop.

JIMMY SWAGGART

The '80s had started out so sweet. Jimmy Swaggart was broadcasting a daily Bible study and music show. His weekend shows were often televised from on-location crusades he held in major cities. Soon, more than 3,000 TV stations and cable systems were carrying his telecasts each week. He had hundreds of millions of viewers and an income from contributions of $150 million a year. Then in 1986 he exposed Marvin Gorman, a fellow minister, of having several affairs. But Swaggart was living in his own glass castle. The now-defrocked Gorman hired his son to follow Swaggart, and following he did, right to Room 7 of the New Orleans Travel Inn, where Jimmy was "visiting" a local prostitute. To his credit and faced with disgrace, Swaggart met the accusations head-on. He appeared on television and tearfully confessed to having sinned. His church was not convinced. His ministerial license was revoked. A bit harsh, don't you think? I mean the man had confessed. Of course, in 1991, he was caught again with a prostitute. This time he told his congregation that "The Lord told me it's flat none of your business." I bet.

JIM AND TAMMY FAYE BAKKER

They were television evangelists in the '80s, when it was still a lucrative undertaking. Preaching the importance of fidelity in marriage and the evils of greed on their show PTL (Praise the Lord), they set themselves up as the pinnacle of all that was holy and pure. Right up until Jim's secretary, Jessica Hahn, came forward and told of sexual advances, playoffs, and ridiculous spending that made Cleopatra seem frugal. Information regarding mul-

tiple homes and cars, private jets, outrageous salaries, and out-of-control spending was revealed. Rumors flew about, including ones of wife-swapping and same-sex dallying. It all came crashing down and the Bakkers divorced, and Jim even did some jail time. PTL.

Moron of the Week:
The Springfield, Illinois, pastor who had to call 911 to send help because he was handcuffed in the church basement . . . the dispatcher had trouble understanding him because he was wearing a leather hood . . . and had a ball gag in his mouth. . . . Something tells me three Hail Mary's just ain't gonna cut it on this one.

CHAPTER THREE

HOLLYWOOD AND CELEBRITIES

"Happiness: an agreeable sensation arising from contemplating the misery of another."

—Ambrose Bierce

A shameless self-promoter once said, "In the future, everyone will be world-famous for 15 minutes." Nowadays, that's about 14 minutes and 57 seconds too long. Celebrity—we embrace it, we obsess over it, we worship it and mostly, we crave it . . . and why? Because we all desire to be in that pantheon of the rich and famous—even if it has all the substance of a soap bubble in a windstorm. It's hardwired in our DNA. (Hey—checking my watch . . . it's 15 minutes *and* counting. Fame is calling.)

MARILYN MONROE

Poor thing, she just wanted to be loved. Hugh Hefner loved her. The first readers of Playboy *really* loved her. Her fans adored her. Joe DiMaggio and Arthur Miller loved her AND married her. John and Bobby Kennedy secretly loved her. And finally, someone loved her so much they administered enough drugs into her system that she died as the result of acute barbiturate poisoning. Everybody loved her—and everybody got just what they needed from her and then discarded her like Jack Lemmon's wig in *Some Like it Hot*. Yep, nobody's perfect.

FRANK SINATRA

The premiere song stylist of the twentieth century started life as a skinny Italian saloon singer in Hoboken, NJ. But you needed help to get ahead. His outstanding attributes included his voice and his charisma. (It was Ava Gardner who described the "other" impressive thing, when she said Sinatra was "only 110 pounds, but 10 pounds was …" let's say Italian salami.) The bars and clubs were heavily infiltrated by the mob. A young Italian kid had to stay on the right side of the powers that be. Those relationships would end up being Sinatra's curse. In the '60s, he tried to cozy up to the new president through Kennedy's brother-in-law and Rat Packer, Peter Lawford. In the '70s, he helped pay Vice President Spiro Agnew's legal fees and he organized Ronald Reagan's Inaugural Gala in the '80s.

But every time he thought he was close to getting the respectability that could garner an appointment to some classy ambassadorship, someone would trot out that infamous photo of Sinatra backstage at the Westchester Premier Theater. There he was all smiles with his arm draped over capo di tutti capi Carlo Gambino, and surrounded by Jimmy "the Weasel" Fratianno, Richard "Nerves" Fusco, and others whose names ended in vowels. Suddenly the White House switchboard would start dropping his calls. It hardly seemed fair. He just sang for those guys. I'm betting on the way to the Oval Office those guys did plenty more.

EVEL KNIEVEL

I just never got the whole daredevil thing. Evel (his real name was Bob) had sought out thrills from an early age and over the years, had participated in everything from rodeos to ski jumping. Things would change in 1967 when he jumped the fountains at Las Vegas' Caesar's Palace on a motorcycle. ABC-TV had bought the rights to the film and Evel was on his way. Of course, the accident that occurred at the end of the jump caused him to suffer a host of serious injuries, including a concussion that kept him in a coma for twenty-nine days. Heck, just the price of fame. In 1968, he crashed attempting to jump his bike over fifteen cars and

broke his leg and foot. Later that year, he lost control of his bike during a stunt, crashed and broke his hip—again. This became the pattern. While we all remember him for his colorful costumes and outrageous motorcycle stunts, Evel Knievel was listed in the *Guinness Book of World Records* for . . . surviving the "most bones broken in a lifetime." So now we know . . . the price of fame: 433 broken bones!

PAMELA ANDERSON

. . . or should I say, Pamela Anderson Lee Rock Salomon. She's had more bad boys between her legs than a jungle gym at a reform school. After appearing as Playmate of the Month in February 1990, Pam decided to get bigger tits and an acting career. The tits are still there. Playing against type as a blonde bimbo on *Home Improvement*, *Baywatch*, and *Stacked*, she became a best-selling novelist with her 2004 book, *Star*, which came with a nude portrait of her on the inside of the dust jacket. But it was her personal life which truly set her (legs) apart from the masses. In 1995 she married Motley Crüe drummer Tommy Lee. A sex tape of their honeymoon was released on video, which posed the question, "How can a man who resembles a human tripod shake the camera so badly?" A sex tape of Pam with Poison musician Bret Michaels was released shortly after. Trying to escape her past and move forward, she then married and quickly divorced "Cocky" recording artist Kid Rock. She reached her penultimate achievement in the bad-marriage tournament with a four month marriage to Rick Salomon in 2007. It was Salomon who filmed and likely leaked the sex tape of him and his then-girlfriend Paris Hilton. After attempting to sue the Hilton family for allegedly tarnishing *his* reputation (WHAT!), Salomon began distributing the film, now called *1 Night In Paris*. Anderson, meanwhile, has just finished a stint on *Dancing with the Stars*.

KATE MOSS

Moss was making millions as the Model Du Jour. She parlayed her look of heroin chic into the norm for other models of the day. Most women could never attain the look, but Moss pulled it off and was admired for it . . . until she was videotaped snorting coke and was

subsequently fired by many of her sponsors. And those same women scoffed, "Of course, how else?" She has since made a comeback, but there was a long moment when the world was gathering no Moss.

PARIS HILTON

Her spoiled rich kid story is the one that inspired the title of this book. Born with a platinum spoon in her mouth, she hit her teens and seemed determined to flaunt her privileged upbringing to the entire world. Up until she got stopped for a DUI . . . while driving on a suspended license . . . and doing 70 in a 30-

mph zone. At her trial she blamed it all on her publicist. She was given a 45-day sentence in jail. Needless to say, it wasn't a penthouse suite.

KIM KARDASHIAN

This is too easy. Kim Kardashian is part of a trio of sisters that make the Gabors look like the Barrymores. Having virtually no talent and absolutely no reason for garnering any public awareness, Kim *"broke"* out in the media for being the spread-legged bimbo beneath Snoop Dog's cousin, Ray J, in an explicit sex video. In a time when explicit sex videos were becoming the equivalent to showing off baby photos, Kim "rode" this puppy into a multi-million-dollar empire. First she sued and won $5 million—making her the best-paid porn star of all time. Then she leveraged her *pubic*

visibility with the E! reality TV series, *Keeping Up with the Kardashians.* Surprisingly, this freak show didn't stop with the video of sexual acts still illegal in 19 states. It turns out that her dad was a friend, lawyer, and suspected accomplice of O. J. Simpson in the brutal murder of his wife, and that her stepdad is gold medal winner Bruce Jenner, who has had more plastic surgery than all the *Real Housewives of Beverly Hills* put together. However, in the true spirit of the Teflon celebrity, Kim's popularity continues to grow nearly as fast as her prodigious backside. A 72-day publicity-stunt wedding, and a class action suit against her weight-loss supplement has tagged Kim as being the poor victim. With the announcement that she gave birth to Kanye West's baby, this Rapper's Delight continues to do her best work with her toes pointed to the ceiling.

CHAPTER FOUR

MEDIA

"People seem to enjoy things more when they know a lot of other people have been left out of the pleasure."

—Russell Baker

And now we come to the real stuff. The world where we all live in big houses, drive fancy cars, have beautiful spouses and there are 2.5 murders every 5 seconds. But the sad truth is that we have to work hard at ignoring the man behind the curtain, because the objects of our adulation don't just have feet of clay, they are a freakin' statute made of silly putty. Every dashing captain, loveable rogue and flirtatious girl next door disguises a coke-snorting, illiterate whore who can shed their image faster than the light changes during Hugh Grant's oral sex. Ok, maybe not everyone . . . maybe . . .

Movies

CHARLIE CHAPLIN

In 1924, Charlie Chaplin's Little Tramp was one of the world's most beloved stars. Few knew he was also the Little Pedophile. While working on his film *The Gold Rush*, Charlie became obsessed with his female star . . . his fifteen-year-old female star. Before the movie was finished, Lita Grey became pregnant with thirty-five-year-old Chaplin's child. Facing prosecution for statutory rape, Chaplin married Lita and they were soon the proud parents of Charlie Jr. A year later, Sydney was born. But there was soon trouble in paradise and three years later, Lita filed for divorce charging the Little Pervert with "abnormal, unnatural, perverted and degenerate sexual desires," adultery and abandonment. Despite the support of many powerful and influential friends, Lita got a divorce on the grounds of extreme cruelty. Her $850,000 settlement was the largest of the time. Smile, though your heart is breaking.

HOWARD HUGHES

It must be having all that money . . . makes you crazy. Successful businessman, movie entrepreneur, inventor, pilot—how does the man who set multiple world air-speed records AND designed a special bra for Jane Russell to wear in the film *The Outlaw* end up being a malnourished recluse, weighing 90 pounds, with uncut hair, beard and fingernails? This was a man who had dated Bette Davis, Ava Gardner, Olivia de Havilland, Katherine Hepburn, Ginger Rogers and Gene Tierney. He asked Joan Fontaine to marry him—twice. And yet, he died alone, five broken-off hypodermic needles in the flesh of his arms from drugs he took to help with his chronic pain . . . and no will. His $2.5 billion estate was eventually split among twenty-two cousins. Apparently none of whom had ever been there to offer help to their now-deceased benefactor.

MABEL NORMAND

A huge silent film star whose career pretty much ended after the murder of director William Desmond Taylor. She was his friend, his lover, and a suspect. Revelations about drug and alcohol problems tarnished her career, and she was involved in another scandal a year after the first one, this one involved the shooting of a lover by her chauffeur. She was out of films after audiences lost all interest and

died penniless in 1930 at the age of thirty-eight.

THE M&M GUY

In 1982, The Mars Candy company was approached by a filmmaker who wanted to use their M&M candies prominently in his new science fiction movie. It was to be the alien's favorite snack. Without reading the script, the Mars company passed. The director then went to The Hershey Company. Though maybe they could let him use Hershey's Kisses. Hershey thought it was possible, but asked Steven Spielberg if he thought his E.T. might be interested in their new product—Reese's Pieces. Within two weeks of E.T.'s release date, Reese's Pieces' sales tripled. They remain one of Hershey's most popular candies. One can only wonder what happened to that guy at the Mars company. Hopefully he phones home every now and again.

JAMES CAAN

In *The Godfather*, when Sonny Corleone, played by James Caan, discovers that his saintly sister Connie was beaten by her husband Carlo, Sonny turns more shades of red than Yosemite Sam. Then he goes to look for Carlo. When he finds him, Sonny chases him down the street, kicking, punching, and biting him. Finally, Sonny brings him down and empties a trash can on him. For good measure, he then hits him with the empty trash can. We loved it. But Carlo gets the last laugh. Sort of.

DAVID CARRADINE

Originally named John, after his B-movie actor father, "David" Carradine found his greatest identity as the Chinese-American warrior monk Kwai Chang Caine on 1970s TV series *Kung Fu*, a concept created by and for Chinese-American martial artist and actor, Bruce Lee. Carradine was born in Hollywood. In an attempt to follow his illustrious father's footsteps, Kwai, I mean David, would return to *Kung Fu* time and time again like a fame junkie looking for a fix. Quentin Tarantino attempted to revive his fading career by casting him in *Kill Bill,* volumes 1 and 2. Despite lots of unrealized Oscar "buzz," Carradine was able to parlay these starring roles into a voice-over on the Nickelodeon cartoon series, *Danny Phantom.* Carradine was soon found hanging naked from a rope in a Thailand hotel room, a victim of what is believed to be "accidental asphyxiation," which in this case was as much of an oxymoron as Carradine's most identifiable persona.

JOAN CRAWFORD

After refusing to eat her dinner the night before, we all knew Joan Crawford's kid was going to be looking at that cold piece of meat the following morning. But getting yelled at for wire hangers? We scratched our heads at her priorities and cherish the fact that Crawford is remembered as much for *Trog* as she is for *Mildred Pierce.*

WINONA RYDER

At the pinnacle of stardom, having just made *Heath-ers*, *Beetlejuice*, and *Reality Bites*, the world was Winona Ryder's oyster. Right up until she got caught shoplifting and her mug shot was everywhere. Her career nosedived. Yes, reality certainly does bite.

MEL GIBSON

Remember the fun-loving, playful Danny Glover's buddy, Mel? Not the wife-beating, drunken anti-Semite we now know him to be. When was the last time you saw a Mel Gibson movie?

LINDSAY LOHAN

From her impressive career breakout at age ten, Lindsay Lohan would experience dizzying heights before descending so quickly we didn't know if it was the fall or the cocaine that caused her nosebleeds. After critical and commercial success, she became a household name that soon became synonymous with a self-indulgent, dependence-driven, has-been. Multiple driving-under-the-influence incidents and numerous visits to courtrooms and subsequent rehab facilities left her little time to pursue acting, which had now become little more than a hobby. So we found ourselves stunned to learn she had been tapped to play Elizabeth Taylor in a TV bio flick. Granted, we were remembering the Elizabeth Taylor of *National Velvet* and Montgomery Cliff and not the creepy circus picture of Liz with Liza Minnelli and Michael Jackson. So we were thrilled when the reviews were universally bad and the movie drew less than a third of the ratings of the Season 3 debut of *Duck Dynasty*. They need to pay the ducks more.

MICHAEL OVITZ

"That package was way too lucrative for the services performed."

Michael Ovitz was *the* uber-agent in Hollywood. After leaving the William Morris Agency, Ovitz co-founded the Creative Artists Agency (CAA) in 1975. Over the years Ovitz represented Tom Cruise, Dustin Hoffman, Kevin Costner, Michael Douglas, Sylvester Stallone, Steven Spielberg, and Barbra Streisand. Ovitz was the one who negotiated David Letterman's move from NBC to CBS. He was the undisputed giant of entertainment. Then in 1995 he left CAA to become president of The Walt Disney Company. After a very difficult first year, Walt

Disney chairman Michael Eisner, cherishing his role as Jack, toppled Ovitz from his throne. After his next venture failed, Ovitz attempted to win friends and influence people by blaming his troubles on a "Hollywood cabal led by a gay mafia." You can still find him on Hollywood Boulevard looking to trade his cow for some magic beans.

ORSON WELLES

Wunderkind Orson Welles emerged as the unqualified genius of the day with his Mercury Theater Production of *War of the Worlds*. Three years later, his *Citizen Kane* would go on to be what is considered one of the greatest films of all time. Over the next forty-four years, he did everything in his power to make us forget the promise of those early achievements. With only a handful of mov-

ies to his name, Orson Welles passed away as a jumbo-sized pitchman wasting his arresting voice by babbling about wine before its time.

BATTLEFIELD EARTH

Originally published in 1982, *Battlefield Earth* is a science fiction epic (over 1,000 pages) written by pulp fiction author L. Ron Hubbard. Hubbard had a minor career as a science fiction/pulp fiction author in the 1940s. Until he put his writing career on hold to develop a self-help system he called 'Dianetics.' He expanded that into the religious movement Scientology. Hubbard is quoted as saying, "If you want to make a little money, write a book. If you want to make a lot of money, create a religion." Despite this spiritual bedrock, the Church of Scientology has attracted a number of celebrities, including Kirstie Alley, Lisa Marie Presley, Tom Cruise, and John Travolta. It was Travolta who had tried for years to bring Hubbard's "masterpiece" to the screen. Finally, in 2000, he succeeded. Directed by Roger Christian (who had been the Art Director for *Star Wars IV* and *Alien*) *Battlefield Earth* was a major commercial failure and critical disaster. It routinely appears at the top of "the worst films of all time" lists. Not only did Travolta produce and star in this disaster, he apparently sunk millions of his own money into it. At least he put his money where his mouth was. He should have started a religion.

THE FIRST *FANTASTIC FOUR* MOVIE

And not the one you're thinking of. . . . In 1986, German-based Constantin Films bought the movie rights to the Marvel comic book characters, the Fantastic Four. As the superhero blockbuster movie era was about to begin, Constantin realized that they were sitting on a gold mine. The only problem was that, to retain the rights, they had to produce a film by the end of 1992. So they made a movie, a very low-budget movie. It's been reported that the total budget was under $1 million roughly the cost of coffee for most summer blockbusters. They hired music-video director Oley Sassone, who completed the film in just twenty-five days. That summer they released the trailer to theaters, announcing the world premiere on January 19,

1994, at the Mall of America. The cast and director went on a promotional tour showing clips of the film at sci-fi conventions. The only thing they didn't do was release the film. Stan Lee was quoted as saying, "The movie was never supposed to be shown to anybody." Without telling the cast and the crew, this movie was made simply to retain the rights. Ten years later, Constantin Films was among the producers of the $90 million-*Fantastic Four* movie which would go on to earn over $330 million worldwide. Hopefully the original cast got to keep their spandex costumes.

HUGH GRANT

With boyish good looks and a charming personality, Hugh Grant was on top of the world following his performance in the 1994 blockbuster *Four Weddings and a Funeral*. An overnight international star, he had his pick of projects. He went on to star with Robin Williams in *Nine Months*, Emma Thompson in *Sense and Sensibility*, and Julia Roberts in *Notting Hill*. So it came as a surprise when he was arrested in LA for having prostitute Divine Brown perform oral sex on him in his car. Apparently, Ms. Brown wanted $100 to go to her hotel room. Grant only had $60, so they agreed that she would swallow her pride and get down to it on the front seat. Caught up in her enthusiasm, Grant apparently kept tapping his brake pedal, causing his tail lights to flash. That caught the attention of the police. The rest is movie history.

EILEEN BOWMAN

Aspiring actress Eileen Bowman was selected to make her screen debut on national TV opposite a major Hollywood star, and was to be dressed as one of the most beloved children's characters of all times. What could possibly go wrong? It's March 29, 1989, and it's the opening number of the 61st Annual Academy Awards. Eileen comes out dressed as Snow White to sing and dance with Prince Charming played by none other than Rob Lowe. But here's the thing. Lowe was appearing on stage following a nasty sex scandal that had resulted from the release of a video tape of him having sex with two women, one allegedly only sixteen years old. Lowe had signed onto this in hopes that he could put the nastiness behind him. With Snow White? Really? Eccentric producer Allan Carr had come up with the idea, which Bowman said looked like a "gay bar mitzvah." This fifteen-minute number is con-

sidered to be among the worst productions in Oscar history. For this slice of infamy, Bowman was paid scale—about 500 bucks.

JOHN CARTER OF MARS

Edgar Rice Burroughs created his character *John Carter* in 1912. (He would also create *Tarzan* that same year.) In 1931, famed *Looney Tunes* director Bob Clampett approached Burroughs with a plan for an animated feature film based on the first John Carter story, *A Princess of Mars*. Eventually the project collapsed. (Ironically, had he completed it, *A Princess of Mars* might have predated Disney's *Snow White* as the first American feature-length animated film.) In the '50s, celebrated special effects master director Ray Harryhausen expressed interest in making movies based on the books. Then, in the 1980s, Disney acquired the rights for a Tom Cruise project. That went nowhere and the rights reverted to the estate. But fanboys got really excited in 2005 when Robert Rodriguez signed on with Paramount to direct a John Carter film using the same techniques he was employing on his *Sin City* film. Forced to leave the project, Paramount let their option expire and Andrew Stanton, director of the animation films *Wall-E* and *Finding Nemo,* convinced Disney to re-acquire the rights. Finally, after nearly 100 years, Edgar Rice Burroughs' *John Carter of Mars* was made into a film. Disney's marketing department got hold of it. They decided to lose the "Edgar Rice Burroughs" reference. Granted they had a huge success with their animated *Tarzan* movie, but that was Disney's *Tarzan*. (Who remembered ERB anyway?) They also dropped "Of Mars." They should have just left things alone. By the time it was released, the truncated orphaned *John Carter* had as much appeal as white paint on white canvas. Disney lost somewhere between $85–$150 million and studio head Rich Ross lost his job. Note to all aspiring sci-fi writers with hopes of film adaptations . . . set your story on Neptune or Uranus.

CHEVY CHASE

What the hell happened to Chevy Chase? He was brilliant on *Saturday Night Live*, made *National Lampoon's Vacation*, one of the greatest comedy movies of all time, and created the personification of *Fletch* that no actor since has been willing to go up against for a reboot. And then . . . *Nothing but Trouble, Memoirs of an Invisible Man, Cops and Robberson,* and *The Chevy Chase Show,* not to mention a handful of movies that have never even been released in the US. So we were thrilled when he returned to television in the NBC sitcom, *Community.* After a number of very public disputes with show-creator Dan Harmon, Chase quit the show. Chevy, Chevy, Chevy. We don't know what we can expect next from him, but I'm betting *Rent-A-Husband, The Sequel* will soon appear on his dance card.

JACK PALANCE

Starting with his first acting break as Marlon Brando's understudy in A *Streetcar Named Desire*, Jack Palance had a storied career on stage and screen. He was nominated for Academy Awards for his performances in *Sudden Fear* and *Shane.* He starred opposite Paul Newman in *The Silver Chalice*, Lee Marvin in *I Died a Thousand Times*, Charles Bronson in *Chato's Land* and Burt Lancaster in *The Professionals*. He's played Fidel Castro, Long John Silver, Ebenezer Scrooge, Dr. Jekyll and Dracula. In 1992, he finally won an Academy Award for Best Supporting Actor for his role as Curly in Billy Crystal's *City Slickers*. Accepting the award, the seventy-three-year-old Palance dropped to the floor and began to do one-handed pushups. But it would be the 1993 Academy Award ceremony that he is often best remembered for. The 1993 Best Supporting Actress category was an embarrassment of riches—

Joan Plowright for Mike Newell's *Enchanted April*, Judy Davis for Woody Allen's *Husbands and Wives*, Vanessa Redgrave for the Merchant Ivory film *Howard's End*, Miranda Richardson for Louis Malle's *Damage* and Marisa Tomei for the Joe Pesci/Ralph Macchio laughfest *My Cousin Vinny*. Talk about a fish out of water. So you can imagine the surprise when, after reading all the nominees's names, he announced Marisa Tomei as the winner. Rumor was he couldn't make out the name on the card and just repeated the last name he had read. The Academy, not to mention their accountants from Price-Waterhouse, deny that it's even possible for the wrong award to be given out. Yet the rumor persists.

CASABLANCA

Producer Hal Wallis bought the rights to the unpublished stage play *Everybody Come to Rick's* in 1942 and began to prep it for a film version. Julius and Philip Epstein worked on the script for a while, then Howard Koch took over. William Wyler was Wallis's first choice; but when he wasn't available, Michael Curtiz signed on to direct. There are rumors that Ronald Reagan and George Raft may have been considered for the role before Humphrey Bogart got the part—it would be his first as a romantic lead. The film was still being written and rewritten as the production got underway, and when completed, it had less than a spectacular opening box office. It's hard to imagine that despite all that, *Casablanca* won three Academy Awards and appears at the top of every list of the greatest films of all time. Here's looking at you, kid.

BACK TO THE FUTURE

I love the *Back to the Future* movie. Great concept, lots of fun. I especially like the part where Eric Stolz, playing Marty McFly, learns the guitar riffs for "Johnny B. Good" from Marvin Berry, Chuck's cousin. Wait. Eric Stolz? Yep, that's what might have happened if they had gone with their first choice. Stolz had just finished an impressive portrayal of the title character in *Mask*. Meanwhile, Michael J. Fox was still committed to the TV show *Family Ties*. They started filming with Stolz, but the director Bob Zemeckis and producer Steven Spielberg felt something was off. Even though it would add another $3 million to their budget, they decided to recast with Fox,

who would juggle his time between the two projects. It became a huge success and was the top-grossing film of the year. Michael J. Fox became a huge star. And even though Eric Stolz became the director for *Glee,* we still think we like him.

GEORGE LAZENBY

In the early '60s there was only one James Bond, and he was Connery, Sean Connery. From his opening appearance in *Dr. No*, he owned the role with a mixture of charm, sophistication, and brutality. He teased us into thinking he WAS Bond by appearing in the first five films. Then he quit. Overworked, underpaid, loss of privacy—who knows? All we cared about was that the tuxedo was now empty. So Bond producer Cubby Broccoli runs into this guy at his barber shop and thinks,

"Isn't this the guy who stars in the Big Fry Chocolate commercial?" You've got to be kidding. Granted Connery wasn't exactly a mainstay at the Old Vic, but really? In 1969, *On Her Majesty's Secret Service* (one of the best Bond screenplays) came out with George Lazenby as James Bond (one of the worst). The best news was Connery came back for Bond #7, *Diamonds are Forever*, before turning over the character to Roger Moore, who—although he will always be *The Saint* to me—did a decent job. Lazenby had minor roles in a number of films and TV shows and is working on his autobiography . . . apparently willing to live and let die.

in the film adaptation of *In Cold Blood,* and then on television as *Baretta*. He popularized a number of catchphrases like "You can take that to the bank" and "That's the name of that tune," and was often seen dangling an unlit cigarette from his mouth. He was considered difficult to work with and made some enemies along the way.

In 2002, he was tried for the murder of his second wife. He was jailed and denied bail but acquitted at his trial. He has kept a low profile since then but has appeared on the Piers Morgan show and on *Dr. Phil*, often with mixed results. He says he will have one more "great" film role, but that is truly doubtful . . . and you can take that to the bank.

ROBERT BLAKE

Starting out as a Little Rascal, Blake was primarily known first for his role as Perry Smith

PEE-WEE HERMAN

Really? The host of a celebrated and popular children's

show and movie series thought it was okay to go to an XXX movie theater and masturbate to *Nurse Nancy*? Bill Cosby would actually defend Pee-wee by saying the situation was being "blown all out of proportion" . . . a poor choice of words. Pee-wee, who pleaded no contest to avoid a very public trial, had defended himself by saying that according to Masters and Johnson, masturbators use their dominant hand. He was right-handed and the police report said he was "jerking off with his left hand." See, couldn't have been him. He had been wrongly accused. He was also "wrongly accused" for child pornography possession a few years later. Apparently Pee-wee had a knack for being in the wrong place at the wrong time. Still, it's hard not to see that quirky bow tie character now and not feel just a wee bit icky.

FATTY ARBUCKLE

It was just a little party. Some booze (ok, it WAS prohibition), some girls, some sex. What's the problem? The problem is that Virginia Rappe died and silent film star Roscoe "Fatty" Arbuckle was accused of killing her with his weight while brutally raping her. Eyewitnesses claimed that they could hear Rappe screaming from behind the locked door, and when Arbuckle emerged, she lay naked and bleeding behind him. Arbuckle was soon arrested and charged with murder. In the end it didn't matter that after three trials, Fatty was acquitted. He had been found guilty by a higher court. He was banned from film-making and his career, destroyed.

ROMAN POLANSKI

Yes, he's weird. Given, a great director, but still, weird. I mean, it's kind of understandable. As a child he was forced to live in the notorious Krakow Ghetto, he managed to survive the Holocaust, and his mother died at Auschwitz. Later, his pregnant wife, Sharon Tate, was murdered by the Manson Family. But sympathy will only go so far. A forty-three-year man having sex with a thirteen-year-old seems to stop the sympathy train. All the misfortune in the world doesn't excuse it. Add to that the relationship he had with a teenage Nastassja Kinski and a marriage to another woman thirty-three years his junior, the verdict tends to be guilty, guilty, guilty, no matter who speaks out in defense of him.

MARLON BRANDO

The Wild One, Viva Zapata, A Streetcar Named Desire—Marlon Brando was a great actor and one tough guy. So it's somewhat surprising that he had a soft spot for nerdy Wally Cox. Brando and Cox were long-time best friends. They grew up together and shared an apartment when they moved to New York. Now, although there is no evidence to support the fact that they were lovers, Marlon was a confessed bisexual. He would have been a tri-sexual if he thought he could get away with it. In any event, it is certainly fun to imagine a buff Brando in a t-shirt, standing at the foot of the stairs yelling "WALLY." Even that is a more pleasant visual than a man pushing 600 pounds, standing in the middle of his own island, wrapped in a sari and eating a cheeseburger, no?

JOHN HOLMES

Porn star. Over 14,000 sexual partners, men and women both. Lots of drugs. Dealing. AIDS. Oh, my. Surprised? Nope, it's all text book. Just surprised it took so *long*.

RIP TORN

Appearing in Studs Terkel's 1974 oral history *Working,* Rip Torn confessed, "I have certain flaws in my make-up . . . I get angry easily." Really? While filming the 1970 movie *Maidstone,* Torn, unhappy with the film, struck director and star Norman Mailer in the head with a hammer. Dennis Hopper claimed that Torn pulled a knife on him during pre-production of Easy Rider.

Hopper said he replaced Torn with Jack Nicholson after the incident. In January 2004, Torn was arrested in New York City after his car hit a taxi. A video of him cursing at the police and refusing a breathalyzer aired on television news shows. On January 29, 2010, Torn was arrested after breaking into a closed Litchfield Bancorp branch office in Lakeville, Connecticut. He was charged with carrying a firearm without a permit and carrying a firearm while intoxicated, first-degree burglary, second-degree criminal trespassing and third-degree criminal mischief. Angry? Nah. Just bat-shit crazy.

JERRY LEE LEWIS

Rock and Roll's first wild man is best known by his

nickname, "The Killer." With early hits like "Whole Lotta Shakin' Going On," "Great Balls of Fire," and "Breathless," "The Killer" shot to worldwide fame, making over $10,000 a night. Until it was discovered that "The Killer" was married to his thirteen-year-old cousin. Wow. Faster than you can say (or sing) "High School Confidential," Lewis was blacklisted and his concerts were cancelled. He was barely earning a few hundred dollars a night for shows in seedy beer joints. Was it all worth it? Well, let's see. Cousin Myra Brown was wife number three. They did stay married for 13 years and have two kids. Lewis went on to have a total of seven wives. And if that's not enough, two of them ended up dying mysteriously. There was a whole lotta something going on.

ERROL FLYNN

Dashing, debonair swashbuckler Flynn lived a playboy lifestyle. The Tasmanian-born (and clearly the model for *Looney Tunes'* Tasmanian Devil) never met a co-star he didn't want to bed. The thing is it apparently didn't matter how old they were or even what sex they were. After Flynn's death in 1961, he was accused of being a Nazi spy, a pedophile, a drug runner, a companion to L. Ron Hubbard at sex parties and the first man on the moon. Okay, maybe not the last, but Flynn's decadent and perverted lifestyle was certainly bigger than one little planet can handle.

Humor is just Schadenfreude with a clear conscience.
—Friedrich Nietzsche

Television

PRESIDENT JEB BARTLETT

After President Bartlett keeps his MS hidden, truly believes that his secretary's death is God's punishment for his vanity and . . . wait, Bartlett isn't real. It is Martin Sheen. I sometimes forget that he wasn't the real president. You know, if you walk like a duck, and quack like a duck. . . . Politics and government of the last twenty years would have been so much better had Aaron Sorkin been allowed to write it. I wouldn't have even minded breaking for commercials.

SOUPY SALES

As host of the *Soupy Sales Show* on WNEW-TV in NYC, Soupy Sales introduced kids to the world of puppets when Kermit was still a figment in Jim Henson's mind. White Fang, Black Tooth and Pookie the Lion shared the stage with guests that included Frank Sinatra, Tony Curtis, Jerry Lewis and many other stars of stage, screen and music. He also claimed that he had been hit in the face with more than 20,000 cream pies during his career. But it was New Year's Day in 1965, that earned Soupy an extra special asterisk next to his name. Ticked off that he had to work on the holiday, he asked his young viewers to go into their parents' room and remove those "funny green pieces of paper with the pictures of U.S. Presidents" from their pants and pocketbooks. He then told them to put them in an envelope and mail them to the studio. Several days later he apologized on the air, said that he had been joking and that whatever money had been sent would be donated to charity. Parents complained and Sales was suspended for two weeks . . . but could never get the egg . . . err, pie, off his face.

TEX ANTOINE

Tex Antoine was a popular TV weatherman for almost thirty years. But in 1968 WABC-TV created *Eyewitness News,* which was to be to the then-current Walter Cronkite-type of news what the *Beverly Hillbillies* was to *Masterpiece Theater.* Wearing matching blazers with a large encircled 7 on the pocket, the anchors were encouraged to be personalities and not just present the news. They were expected to exchange personal comments between stories, or what would come to be known as "happy talk." On November 24, 1976, Tex started his weather broadcast with an ill-fated attempt at a humorous segue. Hearing that the previous story had something to do with rape, he started by saying, "With rape so predominant in the news lately, it is well to remember the words of Confucius: 'If rape is inevitable, lie back and enjoy it.'" What Tex apparently never heard was that it was the violent rape of a five-year-old girl. That was the end of Tex Antoine's career.

CONAN O'BRIEN

Conan O'Brien started his climb to late-night insignificance as the President of the *Harvard Lampoon* while still attending Harvard University. Soon he was added to the staff of *Saturday Night Live* and then, in 1993, as a virtual unknown to the viewing audience, took over for David Letterman as host of the *Late Show*. Initial reviews were not very encouraging

(the *Washington Post* called him "Conan O'Blivion") and NBC was not particularly happy (Greg Kinnear was on speed dial). But slowly the show improved and it began to compete with its competitors for ratings. The cast even won an Emmy Award. Then in 2009, as part of the contract he had negotiated with NBC back in 2004, Conan O'Brien replaced Jay Leno as host of *The Tonight Show*. Unfortunately Jay didn't want to go. Oh, he said he did, and the network gave him this kind of weird hour-long show, five nights a week airing at 10:00 p.m., but he was simply waiting for the snake charmer to set down his pipe and lean over for some curry rice. Then he would strike, and strike he did. On January 21, 2010, Conan was gone from *The Tonight Show* and Jay was back. Of course, Conan got a fair amount of change to allow the return of the chin, but he had the golden apple of comedy snatched from his grasp. What to do? What to do? First thing . . . Twitter. Then go on a talk show bitch tour ("I was just trying to figure out what happened"); (the Legally Prohibited from Being Funny on Television Tour); and then finally re-emerge as a nighttime host on . . . TBS! Yes, TBS, the home of reruns you don't care about and George Lopez—oh, wait, they cancelled him. Conan has a contract through 2015. He'll then be replaced by another rerun episode of *The Jeff Foxworthy Show*. I'm sure at that point the ratings will soar.

DAVID CARUSO

David Caruso exploded on the small screen as the riveting Detective John Kelly on *NYPD Blue*. He was an instant star. He was named one of the six new stars to watch in the 1993–1994 television season. And he won a Golden Globe Award. How did he repay all this adulation and popularity? When his salary demands were not met, he left the show after only four episodes of season two. *TV Guide* would later rank this as the sixth biggest blunder in TV history. Caruso got to watch his big-screen roles fizzle and *NYPD Blue* become the longest-running primetime drama on ABC without him.

BOB CRANE

Turns out that the loveable rogue Colonel Hogan was a closet perv making secret sex films, and Sergeant Schultz was only one of the few who "saw nothing—NOTHING." The rest of us saw way too much.

WONDER WOMAN

While Marvel Comics seems to spit out blockbuster superhero movies like a well-oiled machine, DC Comics can't seem to get out of their own way. Sure, they've had success with repeated reboots of their platinum properties, Superman and Batman. But they have not had any luck in extending that into the next tier of heroes. Wonder Woman is perhaps the best example of this. DC turned down a draft of a screenplay written by Joss Whedon. You know, the guy who's responsible for writing and directing *The Avengers*, which became the THIRD HIGHEST-GROSSING FILM OF ALL TIME, bringing in over $1.5 billion worldwide! *The Dark Knight Rises* is number eight. Then there was David Kelley's TV pilot that got turned down and never aired. Talk about your performance anxiety. Now there's talk of a CW television series depicting a *Smallville*—like approach to a young Wonder Woman. And that's already been delayed once. Good chance we'll be watching *Avengers 10* before we'll ever see a trailer for a *Wonder Woman* movie.

STAR TREK

It's sometimes hard to remember how difficult it was to get the original *Star Trek* out the door—even if that door opened sideways and went "Spfffff." First CBS passed on the concept. They had their own sci-fi project and weren't interested. And that project was named . . . Moe Green; no, sorry, it was called *Lost in Space*. NBC liked the idea of *Star Trek* but of course they wanted some changes. The ship's first officer Number One was a woman. A woman in a command role? That would never happen. And I mean they meant *never*—the show is set during the 2260s. So the detached, unemotional second-in-command was shifted to science officer Mr. Spock. His problem was that he had a slightly reddish hue. With his pointed ears and eyebrows NBC brass thought he looked too demonic. So he was given a slight yellow-green tint—which of course the technicians who were not in the loop kept trying to correct. Oh, and the Captain? Lose Jeffrey Hunter, add William Shatner. Despite all this tinkering, the show's ratings remained lackluster. After three seasons, NBC cancelled *Star Trek.* They replaced it with the pedestrian drama, *Bracken's World,* which disappeared without a trace after a season-and-a-half. *Star Trek* would go on to spawn 5 television series, 12 movies, and countless games, toys and books over the next 44 years … live long and prosper.

GEICO CAVEMAN

Over the years we have fallen in love with many TV commercial pitchmen: the Metrosexual Mr. Clean, the OCD-inflicted Mr. Whipple squeezing his Charmin, and the disheartened and probably heavily-medicated Maytag repairman. Not to mention a menagerie of Clydesdales, dogs, polar bears, frogs, and geckos, the latter being one of the most successful campaigns ever run by the Geico insurance company. Geico had the distinction of running a competing ad campaign at the same time. So while we were being inundated with geckos, Maxwell the Pig, Peter Frampton and Esteban, Geico was also running ads featuring a Neanderthal cavemen with the tag, "so easy a caveman could do it." But it came as a real surprise when ABC decided these thirty-second second commercials would make a great television series. *Caveman* debuted on October 2, 2007. Six episodes later it was gone (there are seven episodes that remain unaired). The New York Post declared the show "extinct on arrival." Geico had the last laugh. They ran a commercial of the cavemen watching the show. Their response? One blows a raspberry!

THE SECRET DIARY OF DESMOND PFEIFFER

Every year the networks unveil their fall schedules and there are always a few shows that cause us to scratch our heads. Shows like the musical dramas *Cop Rock* and *Viva Laughlin*, sci-fi missteps like *Manimal*, and the Siegfried & Roy-inspired animation *Father of the Pride*. But the *Secret Diary of Desmond Pfeiffer* had its own special place on this list. In 1998, fledgling channel UPN announced this light-hearted take on . . . slavery. Yes, you heard it right. Desmond Pfeiffer, played by Chi McBride (a terrific actor), is a black Brit who is kidnapped and sent to the US as a slave, where he ends up becoming President Lincoln's valet. Episodes included stories where Lincoln was engaged in "telegraph sex," dressed in drag and had a body double for Mary Todd's needs. All that was missing was a narration by Alistair Cooke and a cameo from Mel Gibson.

COP ROCK

Before Chuck Lorre, Jerry Bruckheimer and Dick Wolf, Steven Bochco was THE name in television. Bochco was responsible for *Hill Street Blues, LA Law, Doogie Howser,*

MD (with a very young Neil Patrick Harris), and *NYPD Blue*. And while he usually had his finger firmly planted on the pulse of the American public, there were a few days when he must have been wearing bulky gloves. One instance was the comedy-drama *Bay City Blues* which cast Bochco-favorite Dennis Franz as a ball-scratching minor league ball player. Four episodes aired before the series disappeared. But the finest example of the oven-mitt wearing Bochco was *Cop Rock,* which combined police procedural with musical theater. Yes, *musical* theater. Juries in courtrooms broke out in Gospel-style verdicts, cops sang to perps, and suspects got solos along with their Miranda rights. The final episode had the cast breaking character and joining the crew for a rousing final song. (It also featured Sheryl Crow as one of the back-up singers.) It made *Glee* look like *Les Miz*.

BAYWATCH

Baywatch debuted on NBC in 1989. It starred thespian David Hasselhoff. Set on a California public beach, the stories revolved around a dedicated team of lifeguards who routinely saved lives and dealt with everything from earthquakes to serial killers. This was high drama and we were riveted to the non stop intensity of each episode. It was *Masterpiece Theater* with sand. Oh, and there were some fairly well-endowed young female lifeguards in tight red swimsuits who found it necessary to run *everywhere*. After one season, NBC cancelled it. WHAT!!! WHY??? What were they thinking? I mean, all I can think of is that they were afraid of a class action suit by all the young men who had permanent neck damage from rocking their heads up and down repeatedly during each show. Anyway, they did. Gone. No beach. No sun. No neck injuries. Then the gods smiled and *Baywatch* went into first-run syndication for TEN YEARS! It became the most watched television show in the world. And made blockbuster stars of Erika Eleniak, Nicole Eggert, Yasmine Bleeth, Gena Lee Nolin and Pamela Anderson. Ok, not so much. But they were fun to watch.

JULIUS LAROSA

In the 1950s no one had more influence on radio and television than the folksy, ukulele-playing Arthur Godfrey. Godfrey hosted a popular morning CBS radio show AND a Wednesday night variety show on CBS-TV.

While doing his annual Naval reserve duty he had discovered a young singer named Julius LaRosa, who was still in the Navy. Godfrey offered him a job when he got out. In 1951, LaRosa became a regular on the *Arthur Godfrey Show.* He immediately became a breakout star and soon began receiving more fan letters a week than Godfrey. That did not go over well with the megalomaniacal Godfrey. The breaking straw in their relationship came when LaRosa hired Tommy Rockwell as his manager. Control-freak Godfrey *persuaded* his stars not to hire their own managers or booking agents. He preferred his staff to coordinate and negotiate on their behalf. So he was not happy that LaRosa had ignored his wishes. On October 19,1953, following Julius LaRosa's performance of "Manhattan," Godfrey calmly announced to the radio audience, "That was Julie's swan song with us. . . . He goes now, out on his own." He had fired him on the air. LaRosa had no idea it was coming.

Music

FREDDIE MERCURY

Were we really that naïve? Flamboyant, way too handsome, metro-sexual (before that was even a term) Freddie Mercury pranced around on stage, showing off his "junk" under tight pants while performing with his band that was called . . . wait for it . . . Queen.

And we were still shocked when he died from AIDS and it was revealed he had a long-time relationship with a male hairdresser. Could he have been more obvious? Maybe if the song had been called "Fat-Bottomed Guys."

DECCA RECORDS

On January 1, 1962, Paul McCartney, John Lennon, George Harrison and Pete Best were auditioned by Decca Records producer Tony Meeham. The Beatles performed a combination of covers and originals. Shortly after, Decca passed, saying that "guitar groups are on the way out." They did sign another group who had auditioned on the same day—Brian Poole and the Tremeloes. Ironically, their first song to hit the charts would be "Twist and Shout"—which had already been released by, you guessed it, The Beatles. The Fab Four would sign with EMI and go on to what you might call some success—they sold over *2,303,500,000* albums. Decca went away.

MILLI VANILLI

At the height of their fame, Milli Vanilli had one of the best-selling records in the history of the music business. They were two exotic looking fellas, replete with dreadlocks and model looks. They won a Grammy for "Best New Artist" and the music world heralded them. The problem? They couldn't sing a note and lip-synced everything. And when the recording they used in concert was defective and began to skip, the jig was up. The people around them began to tell all.

They were (and continue to be) the punch line to a thousand jokes. Their songs were deleted from their record company's catalog and people who bought their discs could get their money back. One band member died in obscurity and the other continues on the Holiday Inn circuit.

GARTH BROOKS

Garth Brooks was the second-best-selling solo artist of the twentieth century (following Elvis Presley), with four of his first six albums selling over 10 million copies each. His musical style allowed him to dominate the country AND pop charts. He broke records for both sales and concert attendance. Brooks was beloved. So of course he decided the time was right to test his fan's patience. He started work on a movie featuring a rock singer alter ego he named

Chris Gaines. To create publicity for the project, Brooks began to make appearances as Chris Gaines. In 1998, Gaines appeared as the musical guest on *Saturday Night Live*. Garth Brooks was the host. This was getting weird. Brooks began talking about Gaines in the third person. The "pre-soundtrack" to the film was released and it was a major disappointment. His dedicated fans didn't know what to do with it, and he sure wasn't attracting a whole lot of new listeners. Soon the whole strange project faded away. Brooks retired from performing for awhile, signed a deal with Walmart, married Trisha Yearwood, and then signed a five-year contract with a Las Vegas casino. But no matter how much more he accomplishes, you know the brooding, hair-in-his-face character Chris Gaines will still be there stealing some of the thunder.

Meekness: Uncommon patience in planning revenge that is worthwhile.

—Ambrose Bierce

SONY

In the war for home-entertainment dominance, Sony clearly had the upper hand. They made the first successful transistor radio and a popular line of home electronics, and also helped to develop the compact disc. In 1975 they released a home consumer videocassette system called Betamax. They entered the market with virtually no competition, but their iron-fisted attempt to control distribution would soon drive rival electronic giant JVC to develop a competing format. And JVC was very generous with sharing their technology. By 1980, JVC's VHS format controlled 70 percent of the US market across hundreds of companies. What can we learn from this? Apparently nothing. Sony repeated the same mistakes in the late 1990s. They owned the personal electronic market with their Sony Walkman. Sure, there was some competition; but everybody had or wanted a Walkman. Then CDs became popular and there was the Sony Discman. Soon after, digital music started to become popular and . . . uh oh. The Sony digital music player used a system that was incompatible with the MP3 format. It was Betamax all over. Apple created the iPod. Apple? What did they know about music? Well, apparently a lot—they promptly ate Sony's lunch. Apple now has over 70 percent of the MP3 market.

Sony? 1.9 percent. 1.9 percent! *ScanDisk* has 10 percent. Of course, have they *now* learned their lesson? Yeah, not quite. They stayed so long with their Trinitron-tube based TVs that when they saw the writing on the wall, it was writing that their competitors had been reading for years. In order to quickly shift production to the booming flat panel TV market, they had to use Samsung parts.

SAMMY DAVIS JR.

There's no denying that Frank Sinatra loved Sammy

Davis Jr. Their friendship goes all the way back to the early 1940s when Sammy was still a kid and singing in the Will Mastin Trio. Over the years Davis and Sinatra became fast friends, with Sammy later becoming a key player in Sinatra's Rat Pack. But apparently there was a line you just didn't cross. Shawn Levy writes in his book, *Rat Pack Confidential,* that Sammy made some offhand comment about him being a bigger star than Frank. When it got back to Ol' Blue Eyes, he was not amused, and you do not want to cross Mr. Sinatra. First he cut Davis from his movie *Never So Few.* Over the next few months Frank refused to talk to Sammy; even refused to be in the same building with him. He was banned from all of Frank's shows. No one was able to intercede. Finally when he felt Sammy had enough, Sinatra let Sammy back in. But he had one final card to play. When they filmed *Ocean's Eleven,* the Rat Packers all got to dress up and look sharp— almost all. Sinatra cast Sammy Davis Jr. as Josh Howard—the garbage man.

PETE BEST

Probably the only musician who is best known for being fired, Pete Best played drums with The Beatles from 1960 to August 1962. His mum owned The Casbah, where The Quarrymen, and later The Beatles, played. When they were about to leave for Hamburg, they officially asked him to join the band. No one knows what happened. Some say he was too good looking. Others say he was too conventional. Reportedly producer George Martin, who had offered them a contract with EMI, was unimpressed with Best on drums. In any event it was left to manager Brian Epstein to call Pete in and say, "The lads don't want you in the band anymore." Pete was out and Ringo Starr was in. For years Pete refused to talk about his time with the Fab Four. Eventually that would change. It also helped that releases of the early music of The Beatles with Pete on drums, especially those included on the *Beatles Anthology,* may have earned him as much as $7 million. And he didn't have to marry Yoko Ono.

GARY GLITTER

Gary Glitter was a British glam rock star in the early 1970s. He had a long string of hits, including the popular anthem "Rock and Roll, Parts One and Two." Not surprisingly Glitter would eventually see declining sales and face drug addition, which often went hand-in-hand together. But this is where Glitter's career took a definitely odd turn. In 1997, he was arrested for having child pornography on his computer, which he had brought in for repair. (How many times does that happen? You'd think they learn.) He was sentenced to four months' imprisonment. Of course he fled, eventually settling in Cambodia. Okay, Southeast Asia is THE black heart of illicit sex trade. Then in 2002 Cambodia deported Glitter to Vietnam due to suspected child sexual abuse. Cambodia didn't want him? In 2005, Vietnamese authorities arrested him for molesting two underage girls. Glitter was tried and convicted. When he was finally released from prison, he returned to the UK (after 19 countries announced they would refuse to admit him). In October 2012, Glitter was again arrested on charges of sexual misconduct with minors. Some guys just never learn.

Books

WILLIAM BURROUGHS

Joan Vollmer was a prominent part of the early Beat Generation. Her roommate at Barnard College married Jack Kerouac and their apartment became a gathering place for other writers of the era, including Allen Ginsberg, Lucien Carr and William Burroughs. Soon Vollmer and Burroughs embarked on a passionate affair. It was a volatile relationship at best, with both of them engaged in many self-destructive behaviors. After returning to Mexico from a South American trip where he had been pursuing a young man, Burroughs played William Tell and aimed his handgun at a water glass balanced on Vollmer's head. Think about this. At this point Burroughs was struggling with an addiction to morphine and heroin. Just what you want in someone aiming a gun at a glass on your head. He shot. He missed. Vollmer died later that day from a gunshot wound to her skull. She was 28. Burroughs spent thirteen days in a Mexican jail before his brother bribed officials to release him, and he was able to sneak back to the US. Time has forgiven him . . . sort of.

EDGAR ALLAN POE

The Edgar Allan Poe we know today is largely the creation of Rufus Wilmot Griswold, an editor, critic and a man with a grudge against poor Mr. Poe. Somehow, Griswold became Poe's literary executor and he worked hard to destroy the man's reputation after his death. In a biographical article called *Memoirs of the Author*, Griswold described Poe as a depraved, drunk, drug-addled madman. Most of his claims were either outright lies or severely distorted truths. Although denounced by those who knew Poe, Griswold's book became the accepted biography—primarily because it was the only bio available and because readers seemed to enjoy the idea that they were reading the works of an "evil" man. To this very day Griswold's lies still impact the way the tragic Mr. Poe is remembered.

RICHARD BACHMAN

There are countless new writers making their print debut

every year. It was no differ-ent in 1977 when the Signet Book novel *Rage* appeared, written by an unknown Rich-ard Bachman. It received very little hype and sold modestly. Mr. Bachman continued to publish strange little books—*The Long Walk* in 1979, *Road-work* in 1981, and *The Running Man* in 1982. When he pub-lished *Thinner* in 1984, there was even an author photo and a dedication to the author's wife, "Claudia Inez Bach-man." In the book, one of the characters described the events unfolding as something that might happen in a "Ste-phen King" novel. Hmmm. That's when Steve Brown, a

Washington, DC, bookstore clerk, began to identify all the similarities in the writing styles of Richard Bachman and . . . you guessed it, Ste-phen King. A little detective work at the Library of Con-gress provided the smoking gun—Bachman was King. To his credit, when Stephen King learned that he had been outed, he called Brown and suggested that the latter write an article about how he discovered the truth. He even agreed to be interviewed for it. Richard Bachman's obitu-ary appeared citing "cancer of the pseudonym" as the cause of death. But like all things Stephen King, the dead don't stay dead. Bach-man appeared in print again in 1996 with the release of *The Regulators,* which was a companion to Stephen King's *Desperation.* In 2007 Scrib-ner published the Richard Bachman novel *Blaze.* And finally, in 2010, Stephen King appeared on the TV show *Sons of Anarchy*. His screen name: Bachman.

If you prick us do we not bleed? If you tickle us do we not laugh? If you poison us do we not die? And if you wrong us shall we not revenge?
—**William Shakespeare**

JIM FIXX

Fixx was a health guru who wrote the best-selling book, *The Complete Book of Running*. In the book, he rails against smoking, gives dieting advice, and insists on users seeking the advice of their doctor before undertaking the tenets of his book. Which he never did, up until he died of a heart attack while jogging. Had he seen a doctor, he might have been forewarned about two clogged arteries that were dis-

covered at autopsy. Irony on a base level.

JEFF SMITH

Jeff Smith wrote twelve best-selling cookbooks and was the host of PBS's very popular *The Frugal Gourmet*. Quite a ride from his first food-related venture—the Chaplain's Pantry, a deli and kitchen supply store he ran while still a United Methodist minister. It's always rewarding to leave all of that behind. Except, of course, when you can't. In 1997 six men filed suit accusing Smith of sexually abusing them when they were teens working for him at the Chaplain's Pantry. Smith denied it, but he settled out of court for an undisclosed sum, but his goose was cooked.

ERICH VON DANIKEN

In the late 1960s, a Swiss author rose to the top of the bestseller lists with *Chariots of the Gods,* which claimed to prove the existence of extraterrestrial life through interpretations of Egyptian hieroglyphics, fanciful explanations of ancient structures and some outright fabrications. What most of us didn't know was that he wrote the first book while awaiting trial for fraud, and his second, *Gods from Outer Space,* while in prison. Nevertheless, Von Daniken's books have been translated into 32 languages and have sold more than 63 million copies. Ridley Scott has said that his film *Prometheus* was inspired by some of Von Daniken's works. I don't believe that. However, there is an ancient drawing of an Egyptian god holding an object which I'm sure is *The Snark Handbook.*

OSCAR WILDE

Another classic eccentric, Oscar Wilde dressed the part, wrote the part and acted the part. He was always decked out in flamboyant clothing. While studying at Oxford, Oscar walked through the streets with a lobster on a leash. His room was decorated with bright blue china, sunflowers, and peacock feathers. Oscar Wilde was, as you might have guessed, the complete opposite of what Victorian England expected a man to be. An affair with Lord Alfred Douglas brought an end to a brilliant career when Wilde was jailed for sodomy. He died destitute at the age of forty-six.

CHAPTER FIVE

ART

"It is impossible to suffer without making someone pay for it: every complaint already contains revenge."

—Friedrich Nietzsche

Some say "Art" is dead. I say, "Yep, you betcha." Still others say, "Thank Gawd!" And I also say, "Yep, you betcha." Because nothing inspires a good case of Schadenfreud like an "ARTISTE" (definitely in ego-caps) on the way down or out. Whether it be Frida Kahlo . . . or Leonardo Da Vinci . . . or Georgia O'Keeffe . . . or Vincent Van Gogh (don't choke on that last name . . . doesn't matter.) In order to rise to the top of the calling, one usually needs to be high up on the a-hole totem pole . . . a womanizer Pablo (Picasso), a self-aggrandizer (Damien Hirst), a pedophile (Toulouse Lautrec) or a shameless self-promoter (Andy Warhol) . . . but at the end of the day, art is in the eye of the beholder. Here's mud in your eye.

MICHELANGELO

Michelangelo di Lodovico Buonarroti Simoni is still a giant in the art world 500 years after his death. His depiction of the natural beauty of the human form is unsurpassed in the art world. Michelangelo celebrated all that is beautiful and you can't help but feel the magnificence of the perfect human form as you view his pieces like the statue of *David*. So it is surprising that history records the Renaissance artist as being a foultempered, irrational, angry prick, who seldom washed or changed his clothes.

was our original Renaissance man—painter, sculptor, architect, musician, mathematician, engineer, cartographer, bon vivant around town, and more. Come to find out Leo was also a chronic procrastinator who never (I mean never) finished a project on time. (He may have been one of the earliest sufferers of Attention Deficit Disorder.) The *Mona Lisa* took twenty years to finish—Michelangelo did the whole Sistine Chapel in only four. The reason we love all those notebook drawings is that most of his projects were never even started. All sizzle, no steak. He would have made a killing on Wall Street.

LEONARDO DA VINCI

It's sometimes hard to remember that there was a Da Vinci before Dan Brown appropriated him for a pedestrian little novel. But Leo

VINCENT VAN GOGH

Ah, the romance! Apparently not having learned that you should say it with flowers, Van Gogh sliced off his entire ear and sent it to a love interest who had jilted him. That'll teach her. Except it never happened. What the crazed Dutchman actually did was take a razor blade to the lower left-hand lobe and give it to a prostitute, whom I'm sure never asked for a "tip" again.

FRIDA KAHLO

Patron saint of the unibrow, feminist icon Frida Kahlo was creative, passionate, and quirky. Her art depicts an obsessive preoccupation with pain. Okay, painting was a type of therapy for her to get past all the misfortunes in her life—an embarrassing philandering husband, three miscarriages and the constant pain that resulted from an early traffic accident. Yeah, you got my sympathy. Of course, on the other hand, she coped with her husband's affairs by sleeping with everybody and everything regardless of gen-

der. I get it. You have a scumbag husband who is sleeping with your sister … that makes it okay to cheat on him with Isamu Noguchi, Leon Trotsky, Nickolas Muray, and a host of others. It's a good thing she had her art or the Seventh Fleet might have been at risk.

ANDY WARHOL

How an advertising artist who painted shoes refashioned the modern art world is the stuff of legends. And that he was able to do it with Marilyn Monroe and Campbell's Soup really pushed the envelope. But that's what little Andrej Varhola, Jr. from Pittsburgh did. Of course he did it as Andy Warhol. Dollar bills, mushroom clouds, electric chairs, Coca-Cola bottles, Elvis Presley, and Elizabeth Taylor were the engines of an art that was everywhere and that no one understood.

Sure, we did our best Woody Allen pseudo-intellectualist imitation to nod at all the right places, but it made as much sense as watching his "art" films of people sleeping. Andy's art was all about being in "the know." Maybe some-one should have been in the "no" and spared the rest of us at the beginning of this insane journey.

SALVADOR DALI

HELLOOOO DALI! How crazy can it get? Not that he had much of a chance. When he was five years old, his parents took him to his brother's grave. Ok? Except his dead brother's name was also Salva-dor and they told him that he was the reincarnated sibling. He can't write his own name yet and now finds out it's his brother's name and, wait, I'm my brother? A few years later, after his mother died, his father

remarried . . . his wife's sister. Meaning his aunt is now his mother. WOW. Kinda ended any thoughts of becoming an accountant. No, Salvador Dali became an eccentric, larger-than-life celebrity who kept an exotic ocelot as a pet, wore flamboyant capes, suffered an exorcism, and confused everyone who could never figure out where the theater ended and the artist began. That his art featured melting pocket watches (some being devoured by ants), rhinoceros horns and eyeballs slashed with a razor, was probably the most normal thing about him.

PAUL GAUGUIN

So we know Vincent van Gogh was, let's say, a "trou-bled individual." Want to bet what his best friend was like? Paul Gauguin shared the starry Vincent's suicidal, self-destructive, alcoholic thoughts and actions. (Oh, and their alcohol of choice: absinthe. Van Gogh also drank turpentine. Explains a lot.) Gauguin was a mess. He claimed that he was of Incan descent. He had an affair with his thirteen-year-old Tahitian model. He ranted about the Church, defending pornography and suggested that he would use the Shroud of Turin for toilet paper. He railed against local officials and the police for their incompetence. He had no mute button. Before beginning a three-month prison sentence for his attacks on the local "gendarmes," Gauguin died penniless, his body racked by alcoholism and syphilis.

PABLO PICASSO

Picasso collected lovers the way some people would eventually collect his art, and he spent vast sums of money on prostitutes. So why is it that when I see his depiction of the female body in his art I feel . . . well, nothing? NUDE WOMAN WITH A NECKLACE? Say what? Where? I hope he didn't see women like that, because if he did I could certainly understand his "blue" period.

JAMES ABBOTT MCNEILL WHISTLER

Not only did he paint one of the most stern, unattractive, and foreboding women in history, he then became forever identified with her as his mother. Thanks for sharing.

RAPHAEL

A talented painter who toiled in the shadow of Michelangelo and Da Vinci, Raphael was quite the ladies man and bon vivant . . . so much so that he opted to hire staff to paint for him while he dallied about in the boudoirs of the

ladies of the day. Other paint-
ers despised him. He died
prematurely after a night of
excessive sex with his concu-
bine du jour, and his art continued to stay in the shadow
of Michelangelo for years to
come.

CHAPTER SIX

POLITICS

"Politics is perhaps the only profession for which no preparation is thought necessary."

—Robert Louis Stevenson

Mark Twain said it best—"Suppose you were an idiot, and suppose you were a member of Congress: but I repeat myself." And that's an insult to *idiots*. Our current day Land Circus Maximus celebrates the thief, the philanderer, the liar, and the incompetent and raises them to demi-god status. And the majority don't have the common sense to keep it all in the back rooms. No, our current crop of lederhosen flaunt it publically, and then deny it in the hopes our attention span is shorter than a blink of the eye. Way too often they're proved right. So here's to the selfless, dedicated, morally-driven leaders of the world—whoever and wherever they might be. The rest are far more entertaining.

Politics seems to be a profession that's rife with Schadenfreude. From Anthony Weiner to John Edwards to Gary Hart to Bill Clinton, one is hard-pressed to choose the juiciest one. But one that sticks out as a kind of template for many of the scandals inspiring our glee is the tale of Washington mayoral candidate, James West, who ran on an ultra-conservative ticket and won. Anti-abortion, anti-sex, anti-gay . . . you name it, he was against it. Making it all the harder to explain the abuse he showered on young boys he found on Gay.com, in the Boy Scouts, or as part of the orientation he established for interns in his office. Ah yes . . . the Wild, Wild West.

GARY HART

In April 1987, Colorado Senator Gary Hart announced that he was going to run for the presidency by saying, "all of us must try to hold ourselves to the very highest standards of integrity and ethics, and soundness of judgment." When rumors surfaced that the very married Hart was having an extramarital affair, Hart was outraged. "Follow me around. I don't care. . . . If anybody wants to put a tail on me, go ahead. They'll be very bored." Hard to imagine, but that was exactly what the Miami Herald did and within the week, they had photos of a young woman leaving his Washington, DC, townhouse. Again, Hart attacked the media for unfairly judging him. The cojones on this guy! It took a photo of the twenty-nine-year-old Donna Rice sitting on his lap on a boat aptly named Monkey Business to get him to admit the affair. It was only days before he dropped out of the race. But that was not the end of it. Obsessed with the belief that he was the injured party and had suffered at the hands of an unjust media, Hart returned to the race in December and competed in the New Hampshire primary where he won . . . 4,888 votes, roughly 4 percent. He is permanently enshrined in the political museum as the patron saint of "listen to what I say, but ignore what I do."

BILL CLINTON

I'll admit it: I like Bill Clinton. There's something about him that you just want to like. He can look you in the eye and tell you a bold-faced lie, and you know it's a lie and you still want to believe him. The problem is that you could take Arkansas out of this Rhodes Scholar, Oxford-educated world leader, but you just couldn't take him out of the trailer-park trollops that he notched his gun with. If he had been satisfied with the blue-haired Georgetown matrons that have quietly serviced the *oral* office for years, everything would have been fine. Instead, this hound dog's perks in the office came from a series of women that looked as though they were rode hard and put away wet. That was the most damning evidence. Lined up side-by-side Paula, Gennifer, and Monica all looked like they shared the kissing booth at the Little Rock County Fair. At least JFK was boffing Marilyn Monroe and Angie Dickinson.

BOB BARR

Barr was known as a sworn enemy of Bill Clinton. The Post said he was the "meanest anti-Clinton pitbull in the house" at the time. His motto? Everyone obeys the same standards and the same laws. It was a sentiment he would repeat over and over during the Lewinsky affair. Leading the impeachment charge, Barr introduced the resolution, wrote copiously about impeachment and harangued Clinton daily in the press.

He was also a big proponent of the moral high ground, having written the Defense of Marriage Act banning gay marriage and laying out the sanctity of hetero marriage. Which he clearly believed in, having been married and divorced two times and now working on marriage number 3. Until it blew up in his face when wife number 2 claimed he had made her abort their child. And after the smoke cleared from the Clinton scandal, polls showed the American public was an even bigger fan of Bill's than before.

HUEY LONG

Saint or sinner? Huey "King-fish" Long served as Governor of Louisiana from 1928 to 1932. His reign saw an unprecedented number of public works programs. Educational institutions were expanded and improved. A system of charity hospitals was set up to provide health care for the poor. In 1928, just before Long took office, the great state of Louisiana had only 300 miles of paved roads and 3 bridges. Long was responsible for massive highway construction, including building the Airline Highway

between New Orleans and Baton Rouge, and an airport for New Orleans. Louisiana had the distinction of having the lowest literacy rate in the country. Long was responsible for a program that provided free textbooks to school children. But what was the true cost of these accomplishments? It was rumored that he used threats, bought votes and did whatever was necessary to get what he wanted. In 1929, when he tried to increase taxes on the production of oil, state opposition was so fierce that the Louisiana Congress tried to impeach him on grounds of corruption, bribery and gross misconduct. Not only couldn't they get the charges to stick, but those who supported Long were given state jobs, cash and other rewards. Those who opposed him had their relatives fired from state jobs. On September 8th, 1935, Long was at the state capitol building trying to get a redistricting plan passed that would oust Judge Benjamin Pavy, a long-time opponent. Long had managed to get Pavy's daughters fired from their teaching jobs and he had also spread the rumor that Pavy's father had a black mistress. At 9:20 pm, Dr. Carl Weiss, Pavy's son-in-law, furious that his wife was being accused of having "black" blood, shot Long in the abdomen, killing him. Long's bodyguards returned fire, hitting Weiss sixty-two times. Of all the people he had crossed in his forty-two years, it was a twenty-eight-year-old doctor defending his wife's honor who ultimately took down the Louisiana "Kingfish."

J. EDGAR HOOVER

We all have those great images of tough G-men taking down the bad guys. Eliot Ness and Al Capone, Melvin Purvis and Pretty Boy Floyd, Efrem Zimbalist, Jr. and Quinn Martin, all real tough guys. All protecting us from the immoral criminal element threatening our very way of life. So it's a bit of a surprise to learn that the head of this organization was a rumored gay cross-dresser, who lived with his mother and carried out a long-time clandestine affair with his protégé and companion, Clyde Tolson, the Associate Director of the FBI . . . they always get their man.

TED HAGGARD

When a male escort accused the Reverend Ted Haggard of paying for sex and drugs, the evangelical decided it was better to fess up halfway and see how that took. He claimed he had indeed bought drugs . . . and gotten a massage . . . but that there was never any sex. After all, this kind of thing could really hurt the book sales for the tome he wrote with his wife on marriage fidelity. And it didn't play well in the light of his advocating the banning of gay marriage. But it was too late. His escort/lover started giving interviews and eventually wrote a tell-all book. Ted resigned from his lucrative post in his ministry and went into hiding, truly haggard from the ordeal.

IMELDA MARCOS

While regularly faced with our own corruption scandals, we need to take a moment to acknowledge the obscene political and financial abuse of the Philippines' First Lady, Imelda Marcos. All others are simply amateurs. While much is made of Imelda's shoe collection, rumored to be anywhere from 1,000 to 7,500 pairs when Imelda and her husband fled to Hawaii after his regime was overthrown, she also left behind 15 mink coats and over 500 gowns. This buying spree included numerous NYC properties (the $51 million Crown Building, and the Woolworth Building, to name a few), a 175-piece art collection with works by Michelangelo and Botticelli, and millions of dollars in jewelry. President Marcos died in exile, but Imelda has the distinction of being the first wife of a foreign head of state to stand trial in an American court. But where else could it have been held? The co-defendant was Saudi Arabian arms dealer Adnan Khashoggi, the bail was posted by tobacco-heiress Doris Duke (who would leave her fortune to a Hare Krishna woman she believed to be the reincarnation of her only son), and the witnesses included actor George Hamilton. All that was missing were the Ringling Brothers. Acquitted of all charges, Imelda returned to the Philippines where she ran for various public offices, faced even more corruption charges, and retained her jet-set sensibilities well into her 80s. Hey, if the shoe fits . . .

MITT ROMNEY

During the 2012 presidential campaign, our favorite Republican candidate, Mitt Romney, made so many tactical errors that we almost had to give up Texas as spoils of war. At one point, Willard Mitt Romney recommended that undocumented immigrants "self-deport." This overwhelmingly "old white guy" attitude led 71 percent of the Latino voters to push Romney into political insignificance. This had followed his response to the pain in Detroit when he claimed that he was a BIG supporter of American-made cars. After all he drives a Mustang AND a Chevy Truck.

But there was more: "My wife Ann drives a couple of Cadillacs." Damn, who needs a bailout? Everybody just go out and buy four vehicles. Mission accomplished. (Wait, had we heard that before?) He was losing the middle class faster than when the shark chewed up Quint's boat at the end of *Jaws*. But he wasn't done. Mitt then accused 47 percent of Americans (all poor, bleeding-heart liberals) of having a dependency on government assistance that came from their victim mentality. Dr. Mitt had identified our problem. Now if those 47 percent would go out and each buy four cars. . . . Happy days are here again. He was rewarded for his insight and political acumen by receiving just a tad over 47 percent of the total votes. During a year of Afghan/Iraq war exhaustion, high joblessness, a shrinking economy and enough political partisanship to make the Cold War look like a group hug, Mitt lost because America had no faith in him. Wow.

DAVID DINKINS

When Dinkins, then-mayor of NYC, was confronted with not paying his taxes for three years, he said, "I haven't committed a crime. What I did was fail to comply with the law." He served one term and lost the next year to Rudy Giuliani . . . he did have the double-speak down, tho.

FORMER SOUTH CAROLINA GOVERNOR MARK SANFORD

When he disappeared for two weeks, it was supposedly to hike the Appalachian Trail, but it was actually to go to Argentina to visit his mistress while using state travel funds to do so . . . and is now considering a Congressional run in his state. He may be running against his ex-wife.

Really, who needs soap operas when there are real-life politicians?

NELSON ROCKEFELLER

Always a bridesmaid, never a bride. Nelson Rockefeller, of the famed Rockefeller clan (patriarch John D. had an estimated wealth of $300 billion in today's dollars—more than Bill Gates), served as New York State governor from 1959 to 1973. A politically-moderate Republican, "Rocky" just couldn't grab that brass ring of the GOP. He sought the Republican presidential nomination in 1960, 1964, and 1968. His final shot came in 1973. Nixon had him on his short list to replace Spiro Agnew as Vice President. Had he picked Nelson, Rockefeller would have become president when Nixon was forced to resign the next year. But Nixon picked Gerald Ford as his VP instead. Probably for being a good soldier all those years, Ford chose Rockefeller to be his Vice President. After a year in DC, "Rocky" had had enough—the party squabbles, the undermining by staff, and the attacks on his wealth. Rockefeller decided not to run for election in 1976, leaving Ford to pick Bob Dole as a running mate. Rockefeller did campaign for the Republican ticket and it was in Bing-

hamton that he responded to hecklers by giving them the finger. I'm sure the direction of this gesture extended well beyond Binghamton. In fact, he probably aimed it all the way back to Washington.

LARRY CRAIG

Once again an example of a US politician who is best remembered for his actions off the Senate floor. Craig was arrested at the Minneapolis-St. Paul airport on suspicion of lewd conduct in a men's restroom. Apparently, Craig engaged in a little "footsie" under the wall of the stall, suggesting that he was interested in "sexual activity." Okay, I don't even make eye contact with other people in the men's room; Craig was rubbing his shoe up against some stranger in the next stall! What the hell was he thinking? And the object of his affection? An undercover police officer. "Of all the stalls in all the bathrooms in all the towns in all the world, you walk into mine." What luck! Craig, who had served in the US Senate for eighteen years, had a record of supporting anti-gay legislation. It makes you proud to be an American, no?

· JOHN EDWARDS

There was a time where Edwards' biggest problem was his haircut. While campaigning for president, it was revealed that he was paying $300–$500 for haircuts, and up to $1,200, when you added the expense it took to get his favorite Beverly Hills hair stylist to join him on the campaign trail. He took some hits from the media, and the late-night hosts had a field day. Who knew what would happen next? In an act that gives self-destruction a whole new meaning, family-man John Edwards fathered a child with former campaign worker Rielle Hunter, then got another aide to claim that he was the father. He eventually admitted the affair, but denied the paternity. There were rumors of an Edwards/Hunter sex tape, which the court ordered destroyed. Hunter later confirmed the affair, and audio tapes of Edwards arranging the cover-up were revealed. But wait, it gets worse. The North Carolina Grand Jury indicted him of six felony charges, including four charges of collecting illegal campaign contributions. Seems he used more than a $1 million in political donations just to hide his affair. Oh, and while all this was going on, Edwards' wife was dying of cancer. His famed hair stylist should have taken his scissors somewhere south of John's little belly. He may have ended up talking funny, but he would have spared us the drama and, who knows, he might have ended up as president.

ELIOT SPITZER

The Sheriff of Wall Street had made a career of wiping out corruption in New York State. His prosecution of Samsung and other computer chip manufacturers resulted in guilty pleas and $730 million in fines. He went after music companies for the illegal compensation of radio stations for playing certain songs and won big settlements with Sony BMG and Warner Music. His office investigated predatory lending practices by mortgage lenders, mutual fund irregularities, and police corruption. He was on a roll. Wouldn't he make a great governor? Most New Yorkers agreed. On November 7, 2006 he beat Republican John Faso with 69 percent of the votes. Of course, if it looks too good to be true, it probably is. On March 10, 2008, the New York Times broke the story that moral crusader Eliot Spitzer had been paying high-priced prostitutes for sex. A federal wiretap revealed that he had had seven or eight "dates" over 6 months and had paid more than $15,000. Investigators believed that over several years he may have paid well over $80,000 for sex. Whoa! He resigned as governor (leaving New Yorkers with David Paterson, whose blindness was not limited to just his sight), and his wife Silda left him (you try explaining to your wife why you paid over $15,000 for sex). What a waste!

DONALD TRUMP

There was a time when TRUMP had credibility. The TRUMP Tower, TRUMP Place, TRUMP International Hotel on Columbus Circle, TRUMP Plaza Casino, TRUMP Financial, TRUMP: The Game, TRUMP The Book, and more and more and more. So how did he end up such a jerk? Maybe it's all the attention he gets from his TV show *The Apprentice* where he gets to rub shoulders with the likes of Joan Rivers, Bret Michaels, Andrew Dice Clay and Lisa Lampanelli. Maybe it's his bizarre friendship with Vince McMahon and WrestleMania. Maybe he's just a jerk. It all really came out when he decided to run for president. (Yep, TRUMP: The President). He demanded proof that Barack Obama was a citizen. He offered $5 million to charity if Obama would release his college and passport applications. He demanded a revolution to replace the electoral college following Obama's re-election (which he retracted once it was shown that Obama won the popular vote as well). What happened to this guy? He went from us laughing about the hair on his head to now wondering if there's really anything rattling around under that bizarre toupee.

PAPA DOC

Francois Duvalier was the President of Haiti from 1957 until his death in 1971. He created a cult-like persona and would claim that he was the physical embodiment of the island nation. He revived the traditions of voodooism, and began to use them to consolidate his power. Duvalier even claimed to be a voodoo priest.

(Which has always been a plus when voting for president.) When he tried to eliminate his political rival, Clement Barbot, Duvalier began to believe that Barbot had transformed himself into a black dog and ordered all black dogs in Haiti be put to death. Made perfect sense. When he was finally captured, Duvalier had Barbot's head packed in ice and brought to him so he could talk to the dead man's spirit. It is estimated that his government was responsible for the murder of over 30,000 Haitians during his reign. Papa Doc was succeeded by his son Jean-Claude, known affectionately as, what else, Baby Doc. Baby Doc was overthrown in 1986 and fled the country. He returned in 2011 and was taken into custody. He is currently facing charges of corruption and human rights violations. Apparently the apple didn't fall far from the dead, lumbering flesh-eating tree.

Moron of the Week:
The New Mexican judge who was forced to resign after he was caught sexting during court proceedings ... "Your honor, could you please wait until I finish my close to bang your gavel?" "Uh, that's not my gavel ..."

WATERGATE

In the summer of 1972, Richard Nixon's operatives broke in and bugged the Democratic National Committee Headquarters at the Watergate office complex in Washington, DC. We have no idea what they were hoping to learn, since there was virtually no way George McGovern was going to beat Richard Nixon in the November election. The five-man team was caught and arrested. *Washington Post* cub reporters Bob Woodward and Carl Bernstein soon learned that cash found on the burglars could be connected to the Committee for the Re-Election of the President (could this be any more poetic): CREEP and the creepy Attorney General John Mitchell. When it was revealed that Nixon had a tape-recording system in his office and taped most of his conversations, the recordings were subpoenaed and there it was—the man himself talking about ways to cover up the break-in. What the hell was he thinking? He should have just dropped his business cards in the Dem's offices thanking them for allowing his people this little midnight adventure. In the end Nixon was forced to resign, Gerald Ford became President, Ford pardoned Nixon, and Woodward-Bernstein forever changed how the press handled the "privilege" of being president.

ANDREW JOHNSON

Talk about living under a shadow. Abraham Lincoln, widely considered the greatest president of all time, chose Tennessee Democrat Andrew Johnson as Vice President. Huh? Immediately Johnson distinguished himself by giving a rambling and, what many believe, drunken speech when being sworn in. When Lincoln was assassinated, Johnson became president. Let's repeat that. Johnson became president, and he began to undermine his predecessor's work and restore the pre-war status quo. The African American issues were seen as a distraction and he allowed the southern states to determine who could vote, and gave them the right to harshly enforce labor "contracts" with their former slaves. Ultimately his battles with Congress led to his impeachment. Some believe that Johnson's presidency set back advancement of civil rights one hundred years. Ironically, it would be another President named Johnson who in 1964 would work to finally deliver on the promises of 1865.

SPIRO AGNEW

On November 17, 1973, Richard Nixon appeared on television and declared, "I am not a crook"—which we would eventually learn was not true. However, it takes on a different meaning when you put it in perspective. Just about one month earlier, Nixon's vice President, Spiro Agnew, had resigned for being, well, a crook. Agnew had been charged with accepting more than $100,000 in bribes, going all the way back to 1962 when he was a Baltimore County Executive. So, while the president is organizing criminal break-ins and cover-ups, our vice president is lining his pocket with petty cash. $100,000 over *ten* years? Talk about working on the cheap. It made us Americans so proud. In his 1980 memoir, provocatively entitled *Go Quietly ... Or Else,* he accuses Nixon and Chief of Staff Alexander Haig of planning to assassinate him if he refused to resign the vice president. You just can't make this stuff up.

Moron of the Week:
Rand Paul, going after Hillary Clinton about Benghazi, said, "The way I see it, it is the worst tragedy since 9/11. And I really mean that." The people of Ct. would disagree. Not to mention military families throughout the country. Maybe if he gets his head out of his ass, he would be able to see better.

GROVER CLEVELAND

Grover Cleveland is the only president to serve two non-consecutive terms. He was known for his honesty, his integrity, and his uncompromising fight against political corruption. So it comes as a surprise that he is best known, not for his administration, or for the city that bears his name (actually the "Mistake on the Lake" was named for General Moses Cleaveland, who oversaw the first survey of the area), but for a racy scandal that broke when he was running for president in 1884. Maria C. Halpin was a thirty-eight-year-old widow with whom he had a brief relationship. Recent biographers have suggested that the thirty-seven-year-old bachelor may have actually forced himself on her at the end of a date. In any event she became pregnant, and when the boy was born, Maria named him Oscar Folsom Cleveland and identified rising political star Grover as the father. Supposedly, when he learned of the boy, he also discovered that the mother's alcoholism was causing her to neglect the child. Mmmmm. What to do? What to do? Cleveland used his influence to have her committed and then paid for the boy to be placed in an orphanage. Cleveland was able to put a positive spin on the whole affair by his very public acknowledgement of this poor judgment error. Although it gave rise to the chant "Ma, Ma, where's my Pa? Gone to the White House, ha, ha, ha!" it may have actually helped him in his election. It keeps getting stranger. Grover's best friend and very married law partner was named *Oscar Folsom*. Was he the real father? And I'm not done yet. When Folsom died, his daughter Frances became Grover's ward and later ... wait for it ... his wife! He must have had a political machine the size of Texas to keep all of this from soiling his reputation.

ANDREW JACKSON

Andrew Jackson would have a challenging presidency. A wealthy slaveholder, he sought to reinforce his power base by appointing friends and relatives to key positions. He forced the relocation and resettlement of Native Americans and enabled the collapse of the Second Bank of the United States. So it comes as no surprise that he was demonstrating this impeccable judgment before he was sworn into office. In 1788, he became enamored with the daughter of his Nashville landlady. Unfortunately Rachel Donelson Robards was in a very unhappy marriage to an abusive and jealous land speculator. When

they separated in 1790, Jackson proposed and the two were married soon after her divorce. The only thing was that she had never actually filed for divorce. So our future seventh president has the distinction of being involved in a bigamous marriage—a fact that the supporters of Jackson's presidential opponent, John Quincy Adams, were quick to point out.

RICHARD NIXON

Nixon's fatal flaw, outside of being a compulsive liar (really, the man lied about things that made no sense whatsoever), was that he thought he could protect all those around him. Like Clinton would do later, he was confident that the bubble around the presidency provided a safe haven for him and those who acted on his behalf. Unfortunately, he had no idea of the doggedness of Woodward and Bernstein (nor the persistent guidance of Mark Felt a.k.a. "Deep Throat"). As the conspiracy began to unravel, Nixon should have cut away his staff and distanced himself from their actions. If he had just said, "I am not a crook—but they are," he might have been able to finish his term.

DONALD RUMSFELD

Rumsfeld and Cheney, Cheney and Rumsfeld . . . they go together like a horse and carriage. Cheney originally suggested Rumsfeld as the US Secretary of Defense, a post the latter would hold under the Ford and Bush presidencies. The two were great together. They totally missed the Osama bin Laden threat, underestimated the hostile reception of the Iraqi people, and led the intelligence community AND the military off

the reservation. Rumsfeld's insightfulness was legendary. He was once quoted as saying, "Osama bin Laden is either in Afghanistan, or some other country, or dead." Really. You don't think he's on another planet? What a moron. And that, my friend, is one of the "Known Knowns"—the "Unknown Knowns" is why the hell did we let them stay in charge?

KARL ROVE

Karl Rove has been a tool for the Republican Party for the past twenty years. (Actually, he's been a tool for all of us.) A protégé of Dr. Frankenstein, Roger Ailes, he was instrumental in blowing up the non-issues that became the game changers that led to the defeat of Al Gore and John Kerry. Rove, who probably is most comfortable slithering across a room on his belly, continues

to be a bully and disrupt the political process through lies and manipulations. The good news is they're saving a special spot for him in the Eighth Circle of Hell.

BUDDY CIANCI

Vincent "Buddy" Cianci, Jr. never lost a mayoral election in Providence, Rhode Island. He also never picked up the soap in the big house, where he served time for racketeering conspiracy—for allegedly running a criminal enterprise. Charges which drove him from the mayor's office twice.

ROD BLAGOJEVICH

In a world where we find ourselves wondering just how corrupt and stupid our politicians can be, it's nice to find a Rod Blagojevich to blow past all our expectations. The former Governor of Illinois was found guilty of seventeen charges of corruption, including the solicitation of bribes for political appointments, one of which was the US Senate seat vacated by President Barack Obama. He was sentenced to fourteen years in a federal prison, eligible for release in 2024. Quite the

reality check for a man who had spent the last days of his freedom appearing on *The Daily Show* and *David Letterman*.

ROBERT PACKWOOD

US Senator Robert Packwood of Oregon resigned after the Senate Ethics Committee unanimously recommended that he be expelled from the Senate for ethical misconduct. Packwood was a pig and there was documentation that he had sexually abused ten women, most of them former staffers and lobbyists. And he kept a diary detailing all his exploits. The man got what he deserved.

GARY CONDIT

Condit served as a member of the US House of Representatives in the '90s. He was extremely critical of Clinton's extracurricular activities and publicly demanded that Bill "come clean" on his relationship with Monica Lewinsky. So we all know what comes next. Not only was the married Condit exposed as having an affair, but he was accused of having an affair with a woman who had just gone missing. Chandra Levy was a twenty-three-year-old intern from Condit's district. After denying the relationship to the police twice, the "pro-family" Condit finally admitted it all. Levy was thirty years younger than Condit and, in fact, two years younger than his daughter. In the end there was no connection between Condit and Levy's disappearance. Just bad karma. His political career was over.

CHAPTER SEVEN

MEN AND WOMEN

"I've already told you: the only way to a woman's heart is along the path of torment. I know none other as sure."

—Marquis de Sade

"When a man steals your wife, there is no better revenge than to let him keep her."

—Sacha Guitry

When it comes to the "Battle of the Sexes," the best advice is to always tread lightly. This is the one place where the Schadenfreude can be more bittersweet that satisfying, especially if the other person is a significant other. As we argue amongst ourselves over power, the fall from grace that is inevitable can often times cause as much damage to the one experiencing glee as it can to the hapless victim. Yes, tread very lightly . . . these folks clearly didn't.

ANTONY AND CLEOPATRA

Looking to gain a powerful political ally after the assassination of Julius Caesar, Mark Antony arranged a meeting with Cleopatra. Although rather plain, Cleopatra was a captivating presence and Antony was instantly charmed. He followed her back to Egypt. This was not particularly good news back in Rome, where Antony had previously wed Octavian's sister, Octavia. Octavian declared war on the two lovers, and soon his naval fleet defeated the joint forces of the star-crossed couple. They fled back to Egypt. Shortly after that, Antony received a report that Cleopatra had committed suicide. Overcome with grief, he plunged his sword into his abdomen. Now, you wouldn't think to ask for a second opinion, some supporting

evidence because . . . you guessed it. Cleopatra? Not so dead. Antony's men took him to the hiding Cleopatra where he would die in her arms. Legend has it she had a poisonous snake smuggled into her cell after being captured, and soon joined her lover as the patron saints of impulsive behavior.

No lover, if he be of good faith, and sincere, will deny he would prefer to see his mistress dead than unfaithful.

—**Marquis de Sade**

HELOISE AND ABELARD

Celebrated French teacher and philosopher Pierre Abelard was Heloise d'Argenteuil's live-in tutor. He was also twenty years her senior. After falling in love, they secretly married and she soon gave birth to their son. Then faster than you can say, "Woody Allen Soon Yi," Heloise's uncle finds out about it and has Abelard castrated. Let me say that again. Has … him … castrated. What the hell is wrong with these people? Abelard becomes a monk, Heloise becomes an abbess, and they begin to write a series of letters to each other until their death. They never met again, which doesn't sound nearly as bad as the fact that he never saw his penis again either.

CATHERINE THE GREAT AND GRIGORY POTEMKIN

Catherine the Great was the wife of Russian Czar Peter III. After only one year in power, Peter is overthrown and killed (probably with just a little bit of help from Catherine). During all this, Russian soldier Grigory Potemkin was the guard protecting Catherine. (Didn't we see this movie with Whitney Houston and Kevin Costner?) Catherine, who would become empress only days later, took a liking to Potemkin and the long-time relationship was a go. Oh, and that Kevin Costner thing? Seems that Potemkin was obese, vain, and missing

an eye. Story is that when their relationship did eventually wane, Grigory became her number one pimp, procuring young soldiers from their barracks for her insatiable appetite. There's no record to indicate he also visited the stables.

(PRINCE) EDWARD AND WALLIS SIMPSON

Edward, the handsome Prince of Wales and heir to the British throne, changed the course of his life, and that of British history, when he fell in love with the married American Wallis Warfield Simpson. When his father, King George V, died on January 20, 1936, Edward ascended the throne as King Edward VIII. After looking in vain for some sort of marriage that would be approved by the Church of England and the British people, he abdicated on December 10, 1936. He had been king less than a year. (A year which included him becoming the first British monarch to fly in an aircraft and also being the target of an assassination attempt. Busy year.) Edward told the world in a famous radio broadcast that he found it impossible to carry the heavy burden of being king without the support of the woman he loved. Give me a break. You're the King of England for Christ's sake. After Simpson's divorce in 1937, Edward and Wallis were married in a small ceremony and spent the rest of their lives in France, where he watched generations of royals pass through the gates of the palace that should have been his. Must have been quite a woman.

LARRY FLYNT

Larry Flynt gave the world *Hustler*. He was a struggling Ohio entrepreneur publishing a little-seen, sexually-explicit magazine, when he acquired and published nude pictures of Jackie Kennedy Onassis sunbathing. He paid $18,000 for them. Within a few days he had sold over a million copies of his magazine and an empire was born. Not as philosophical as Heffner nor as worldly as Guccione, Flynt remained the guy who used to physically beat up rowdy bar customers and toss them to the street. His pictorials pushed the envelope, his cartoons were disgusting, and his articles brought him before the Supreme Court. But he certainly put his money where his mouth is, or, I should say, his legs. In 1978 while appearing at an obscenity trial in Georgia, Flynt was shot by a sniper. This left him partially paralyzed and in constant pain. Years later, white supremacist serial killer Joseph Paul Franklin confessed to the shooting, saying he was outraged by an interracial photo shoot which appeared in the magazine. Confined to a wheelchair for life, Flynt continues to relentlessly publish obscene and provocative material. The only difference? He's gone from pornographer to crusader.

JOEY BUTTAFUOCO

Why in the world do I even know who Joey Buttafuoco is? Because he had an affair with a seventeen-year-old bimbo named Amy Fisher, who then shot Buttafuoco's wife in the face. And if this horror show isn't enough, after serving four months in jail for statutory rape, three years later, Joey pleaded no contest to charges of soliciting a prostitute, spent a year in prison for insurance fraud, and served additional time for illegal possession of ammunition while on probation. The kicker is all this made him some sort of weird celebrity. He's appeared on Fox Network's *Celebrity Box-*ing, CNN's *Larry King*, the *Howard Stern Show*, *As the World Turns*, and in a number of low-budget movies. All because he slept with a psycho teenager who carried a gun. She, of course, became a porn star. Please come get me when their obscene fifteen minutes of fame is up.

Moron of the Week:

The judge in Michigan who was suspended for texting shirtless pictures of himself to his co-workers . . . yeah 'cos that's never hurt the career of anybody before . . . and this guy specializes in sexual misconduct cases. Yikes. At the very least, it shows really poor judgment, no?

Men should be either treated generously or destroyed, because they take revenge for slight injuries—for heavy ones they cannot.

—Niccolo Machiavelli

CHAPTER EIGHT

CRIME

"I have never killed a man, but I have read many obituaries with great pleasure."

—Clarence Darrow

Some say "Art" is dead. Others say, "Yeah, he's dead and I whacked him and he's buried beneath the bleachers at the 50-yard line." Among the giants of crime, a tragic ending is de rigueur—Crazy Joe Gallo's birthday surprise at Umberto's Clam Bar (What to get for the man who has everything? How about a hail of bullets to the torso?); Bugsy Siegel's assassination while reading the *LA Times* (What's black and white and red all over?); or Al Capone's syphilis-ravaged body trying to battle a stroke *and* pneumonia (And you thought Hymie Weiss and Bugs Moran were tough?). They weren't kidding when they said "crime doesn't pay." Our thing (or as the Sicilians would say, "Cosa Nostra") is to show how much it cost.

JIMMY HOFFA

Teamster leader Jimmy Hoffa had a long reputation with organized crime. His outrageous behavior often put him at odds with the unions. Over the years he was convicted of jury tampering, attempted bribery, and fraud for the improper use of the Teamster's pension fund. After serving five years of a thirteen-year sentence, Hoffa emerged from prison AND received a $1.7 million lump sum payment of his Teamster's pension. Of course that was not good enough. He wanted to take back his position of head of the union. The government imposed restrictions against him doing so, and the union leaders in charge resisted turning over control. Now you would think that with close to $2 million you could find something else to keep you out of trouble. Not

Hoffa. He went back to a local Teamster branch and began a campaign to re-establish his power base. And, oh yeah, he announced he was writing his autobiography, *Hoffa: The Real Story*. Top of the world, Ma. What could possibly go wrong? On July 30, 1975, police found his car abandoned in the parking lot of a restaurant located in a suburb of Detroit. His body has never been found despite persistent rumors that he remains a cornerstone in the union, organized crime's architecture.

JOHN GOTTI

Alleged former leader of an alleged Italian crime organization, who, after having supposedly ordered numerous murders and other heinous crimes, was finally convicted and imprisoned for the rest of his life in a US Penitentiary. There the Dapper Don was forced to exchange his $1,000 suits and Italian loafers for prison jumpsuits. He died in 2002 after spending his last ten years in solitary confinement. It's doubtful that the last thing he heard was Journey's *"Don't Stop Believin'."*

Moron of the Week:
The Chicago woman who has been arrested nearly 400 times in the last 35 years. The justice department there is clearly channeling the Cubs and warning her about the "400 strikes and out" rule.

Moron of the Week:
The Oklahoma woman who hid a loaded gun in her "private parts" during a police search. She also had a bag filled with meth shoved up her ass. Kind of like a human advent calendar. On a positive note, Merle Haggard will immortalize her in a new song, "Shooter in her Cooter."

VINCENT GIGANTE

Vincent Gigante, or "The Chin" as he was known by, was the boss of the Genovese crime family from 1981 to 2005. For thirty years, Gigante feigned insanity to avoid prison stays. He would wander the streets of Greenwich Village in his bathrobe and slippers, mumbling to himself. In 1990, a federal court ruled that he was mentally unfit to stand trial. And it was all a lie. In 2003, he pleaded guilty to racketeering charges and admitted that the insanity was an elaborate effort to avoid prosecution. And you thought Robert De Niro was a good actor?

Moron of the Week:
The Las Vegas woman who was arrested for having sex in her front yard with her pitbull . . . evidently, not everything that happens there, stays there . . . so Vegas is changing their motto . . . "Not yet Florida but working hard to get there!" Where's a sinkhole when you need one. . . .

Moron of the Week:
The Upstate New York mother who was arrested after she hired two strippers for her son's sixteenth birthday party. Guess it's hard to top a clown and pony rides when you can't afford to take everyone on a safari.

THE FIRST NATIONAL BANK OF NORTHFIELD, MINNESOTA

It certainly seemed like a good idea. On November 7, 1876, Frank and Jesse James, Cole, Jim and Bob Younger, and a few others of their gang rode into town to rob the bank. They had done similar jobs before. Except these townspeople weren't going to take it. After noticing that something wasn't right at the bank, someone sounded the alarm. As the robbers started to escape, firing their weapons to scare people away, the people started coming out and shooting back. In the end two robbers, a banker and a Swedish immigrant lay dead and all the money remained safely in the bank. A massive manhunt ensued. Soon more of the gang ended up dead or captured. It was the end of the James–Younger Gang.

Moron of the Week:
The Trinidad security guard who accidentally shot off his own penis with an illegal handgun held in his waistband. Well, there go his plans to get his Private Dick license.

BUGSY SIEGEL

Bugsy Siegel created Las Vegas. He was also one of the founders of Murder Incorporated, was a major bootlegger during prohibition, and had a criminal record that included armed robbery, rape and murder dating back to his teenage years. Talk about an over-achiever. This ruthless sociopath was an associate of Meyer Lansky, Lucky Luciano, Frank Costello, Albert Anastasia and Vito Genovese. Powerful men—scary enemies. But Bugsy coasted through it all and was soon rubbing shoulders with the Hollywood elite—George Raft, Clark Gable, Gary Cooper and more. He was a golden boy. Some say he was spending too much of the mob's money on Vegas, others say that he was skimming the profits and he was too showy—whatever the reason, the man who literally created the world he lived in couldn't stop a. 30-caliber military M1 carbine aimed at his head.

Moron of the Week:
The two Australian men trying to break into a high-end jewelry store but misread the plans and instead broke into a neighboring KFC. Hey, they could have used the buckets to haul the diamonds . . . you know, ice buckets? The rest is gravy.

THE BOSTON BOMBERS

These adolescent asswipes used their yet-to-be-developed brains to wreak havoc on the 2013 Boston Marathon for . . . no apparent reason. They assembled an ultra low-tech weapon to inflict maximum damage to gain support for Eastern European immigrants who come to America and get to go to really good schools, party with their friends and end up with better opportunities than their native-born colleagues. Yeah, you keep thinking, Butch, 'cause that's what you're good at.

CHAPTER NINE

SPORTS

"If you make every game a life-and-death thing, you're going to have problems. You'll be dead a lot."

—Anonymous

Ah, to feel the turf beneath our spikes, the touch of pigskin sliding into our grasp, the swoosh of the net—wait, and how much are you paying me? Yes, sport's favorite statistics these days are the number of zeros in their W2s. These heroes of the masses slide from admiration faster than a stool sample after a Taco Bell Beefy Crunchy Burrito. And what's amazing is they land in the proverbial bowl with nothing to their name but an unauthorized sex video. Sports contracts should just automatically give 90 percent of the cash up front to the pimps, dealers and hookers that latch on/latch off to the athlete du jour. Massive egos that dismiss anyone with a clue from their entourage can fill volumes in the Encyclopedia of Schadenfreude.

The sports world has always had its share of pompous jerks and it's no wonder. We spend billions of dollars on it . . . watching it, playing it, buying memorabilia, going to games, sitting in bars and arguing about it . . . and wishing we could do the things that the best and brightest in sports can do, seemingly without effort. So when a sports star falls from the top of the heap, the Schadenfreude overtakes us like Mario Andretti in the last lap at Indy.

TIGER WOODS

Talk about your Golden Boy. A child prodigy, he began playing golf at the age of two. He won the Junior World Golf Championships six times before he was sixteen. At age twenty, he became the first golfer to win three consecutive US Amateur titles. After turning pro in 1996, Tiger Woods signed the most lucrative endorsement contracts in golf history. Sports Illustrated called his playing at the 2000 US Open the "greatest performance in golf history." His win at the 2001 Masters Tournament made him the first player to hold all four major professional golf titles at the same time. Charming and charismatic, he was a hero to young people all over the world. It was too good to be true. No, I mean, it *was* too good to be true. Once Toto got hold of the curtain and exposed the man behind the wizard, there

would be no way to get back to Kansas. Inspiring role model Tiger Woods was revealed to be a serial cheater, having sex with porn stars, models, cocktail waitresses, single moms, and escort girls while his loving wife stayed at home raising their two children. What was he thinking? Were these women really going to keep quiet? Was he going to beat the statistics and not pick up an STD that he could then share with his wife? Did he have any need for all his golf clubs when all he wanted to play was his wood? Well, live by the sword, die by the sword.

O. J. SIMPSON

He had it all. A stellar sports career . . . endorsements . . . a beautiful wife . . . adulation . . . and it just wasn't enough. After a divorce from his second wife where there had been reports of domestic violence, she is found murdered, along with her boyfriend. O. J. is charged. Rather than turn himself in, he leads the LA police on a SLOW SPEED chase, in a now infamous white Bronco. He's eventually arrested and a trial ensues. It's a circus from the jump, with histrionics, grand-standing, ridiculous arguments and weird testimony, while a cloud of politics hung over the proceedings the entire time. He's acquitted ... and the whole world starts to argue about it for the next ten years. He goes underground. He attempts to register his name(s) as a trade-mark. He's arrested for speeding a boat through a manatee pre-serve. And then there surfaces a farcical caper that involves armed robbery, memorabilia, Las Vegas, and ultimately, arrest and incarceration.

used to describe what some say was the greatest who ever played the game. The play-ers who took the abuse he dished out—spitting, cleating, taunts, racial epithets, punches, kicks—you name it . . . they had a different opinion. Not a "Georgie Peach" at all.

> Vince Lombardi said, "Show me a good loser and I'll show you a loser."

TY COBB

Mean. Ornery. Racist. These are just a few of the endear-ing terms that history has

CHAPTER TEN

MISCELLANEOUS

"Neid zu fühlen ist menschlich, Schadenfreude zu genießen teuflisch."
"It is human to feel envy, but it is diabolic to enjoy Schadenfreude."

—Arthur Schopenhauer

In a world where we celebrate the untalented, quote the unintelligent, and vote for the immoral, it still comes as a surprise that there are those who inspire a chronic case of Schadenfreude without excelling in any particular discipline. These are the average jamokes who put their right blinker on and then turn left, hide a ton of cocaine in their unlicensed vehicle, and espouse the right to arm bears (or something like that) while refusing to pay their income tax. Ah, it's good to be an American. The good news is their tales of woe adds a little spring to our every step. So, hop to it.

LAUREN CAITLIN UPTON

Lauren Caitlin Upton was vying for the chance to become the 2007 Miss Teen South Carolina. She was asked a question regarding what her thoughts were on why a fifth of Americans could not locate the United States on a world map:

"I personally believe that US Americans are unable to do so because, uh, some, uh . . . people out there in our nation don't have maps and, uh, I believe that our, uh, education like such as in South Africa and, uh, the Iraq, everywhere like such as, and, I believe that they should, our education over HERE in the US should help the US, uh, or, uh, should help South Africa and should help the Iraq and the Asian countries, so we will be able to build up our future, for our children."

She became a huge Internet sensation.

Moron of the Week:
The Florida man who tried hunting for squirrels by taping a live .40-caliber bullet cartridge to the end of a high-powered BB gun and pulling the trigger. The pellet hit the bullet cartridge and exploded in his face, wounding him badly. Something tells me the whole contraption came in an Acme box.

ADAM WHEELER

Adam Wheeler's application to Harvard University had stated that he had earned a perfect SAT score, had a perfect academic record at Phillips Academy, and that he had studied for a year at MIT. Of course Harvard wanted him. A model student, he was awarded thousands of dollars in financial aid and other grants. Then in 2009 Wheeler applied for a Rhodes Scholarship, which would seem to be the logical culmination of his lifelong academic achievement. If only it was *true*. While reviewing his application, an English Professor at Harvard began to suspect something was not quite right. It was soon discovered that Wheeler had falsified standardized test scores and submitted a fake transcript filled in with A's. On the letters of recommendations from professors that he had used to get into Harvard, he had changed the name of their colleges to MIT from Bowdoin College. Why Bowdoin? Because that's where he really *went* to school. He had never attended Phillips Academy nor MIT

And he had been suspended from Bowdoin for plagiarizing, a practice he continued at Harvard, winning prizes using plagiarized essays. With his academic house of cards about to fall, Wheeler began to apply for transfer to Yale, Brown, Stanford, and other Ivy League colleges. Before that could happen, Wheeler was arrested on twenty felony and misdemeanor counts, including identity fraud and larceny. He was ultimately convicted and sentenced to ten years of probation, a condition of which was that he could never portray himself as a Harvard student or claim that he had ever even attended Harvard. Which of course is exactly what he did on his job application. He was caught and sentenced to one year in prison—where I'm sure he's now the acting warden.

CEDAR FIRE

In October 2003, Sergio Martinez was hunting in San Diego County when he got lost. After deciding not to call out to his hunting partner because he didn't want to "scare away the deer," he gathered sticks and brush and lit a signal fire to attract the attention of rescue workers. He certainly got their attention. The fast-moving dry Santa Ana winds took hold of the fire, and within minutes it was out of control. When it was over almost 300,000 acres were burned, 2,820 buildings destroyed and 15 people killed. Martinez was sentenced to six months in a minimum-security prison, had to perform 960 hours of community service and pay $9,000 in restitution. He was also court mandated to take up fishing.

Moron of the Week:
The Texas woman who saw a snake in her yard, doused it with gasoline, and set it on fire. The snake slid into a brush pile—which promptly ignited and burned her house down. Mother Nature can be one mean bitch.

COCA COLA

For years Coke has denied that their "secret ingredients" included coca leaves (the source for cocaine). Despite boldly proclaiming that "Coke is it!" and that "It's the real thing," we were encouraged to believe that it's all just a happy coincidence. Coke. Cocaine. Sort of like Freddie Mercury fronting a band named Queen. It became a faster tap dance when a Bolivian report indicated that they had authorized the exportation of 159 tons of coca leaves to the US for the manufacturing of Coca Cola. Must be a different US? But controversy is nothing new for the Coca Cola Company. They had to defend themselves from rumors that Coca Cola had collaborated with the Nazis in the '30s, operated racially-segregated housing, workplace and wages in South Africa in the '80s, and even from a controversial 2013 Super Bowl commercial featuring an Arab walking across the desert with his camels craving an ice-cold coke. It's hard to believe such a huge corporation could make so many mistakes—that is until you learn that Coke had the opportunity to buy their biggest rival Pepsi THREE times and passed.

Moron of the Week:
The British man who cooked and ate his own finger after losing it in a motorcycle crash. Huh. Finger food. Must have used that old English recipe for digits and mash.

Moron of the Week:
The Cleveland man who was found with over 300 animals in his house after police received a call about the smell. Other than occasionally feeding them, he confessed to doing

nothing else to care for the menagerie. Asked what he did the rest of the time, he replied, "I do little."

ZIMA

In the 1990s there was a brief "clear craze," where manufacturers decided that the public wanted products to be clear—Crystal Pepsi, Tab Clear, Clear Ivory dishwashing liquid, Gillette Clear Deodorants. Most would soon disappear. During this time the Coors Brewing Company introduced Zima Clearmalt, a lightly-carbonated alcoholic beverage. Not quite "clear beer," it was designed to provide an alternative to the growing wine cooler business. For a while it experienced modest success, and was sometimes used as a mixer in mixed drinks—cool, lets add even more alcohol to our drinks. Coors tried add-ing flavors and even color to Zima to increase its popularity, but it was all over. They stopped US production in 2008.

It is even harder for the average ape to believe that he has descended from man.

—H. L. Mencken

PCBs

PCBs were used as coolants and insulating fluids for transformers and capacitors (you know, those little metal cylinders found in old fluorescent light figures), additives in paint, cements, PVC coatings, pesticides, wood floor finishes, water-proofing compounds, even the old carbonless copy (NCR) paper. They were so versatile—a virtual miracle compound. Too bad they were toxic. PCBs have polluted our environment around the world. In Ireland, PCB-contaminated feed caused the withdrawal and disposal of all pork products produced since 2008. The New Bedford Harbor in Massachusetts is a Superfund site with the highest sediment concentrations found in a marine environment. GE released nearly 1,500,000 lbs of PCBs into the Hudson River, which resulted in a ban on fishing. The cleanup continues after thirty years. Over 2 million pounds of PCBs were dumped in Monroe and Owen counties in Indiana. The authorities are still trying to figure out how to clean it up. Belgium, Italy, Slovakia—the legacy of PCBs continues with no solution in sight. We just have to add "cancer" to the list of all things it's responsible for.

> *Moron of the Week:*
> The Florida woman who was badly wounded when the bullets that her roommate left in the oven exploded as she was heating waffles. "Hey, copper, if dere was bullets in dis here oven, would I shut the door and turn it on? Ya might, rabbit, ya might!"
> Somewhere Bugs and Chuck Darwin are laughing their asses off.

THE ELECTRIC CAR

From the late 1800s through the early 1920s, electric automobiles competed with petroleum-fueled cars. That's right, the *1800s.* In fact, in *1897,* there was a fleet of electric taxis in NYC. The *New York Times* wrote in 1911 that the "electric car was ideal" because it was cleaner, quieter and much more economical than gasoline-powered cars. So, what happened? Well, the government began expanding and improving our interstate highway system (of course, at the expense of our rail lines). This encouraged motorists to drive farther than battery life allowed. No need to take a train when I can drive. I'm in control of my destiny. And gas? Gas was plentiful. There was plenty and it was CHEAP. So, say goodbye to the electric car and hello to the gas-guzzling macadam mobile. Think of where the world would be today if only . . .

HETTY GREEN

"The Witch of Wall Street" was once the richest woman in the world with an estimated wealth of over 3 billion in today's dollars. And yet, to save money, she worked out of boxes at her bank so she didn't have to pay rent. She was constantly moving back and forth from NY to NJ to avoid taxes. She always wore the same dress and never changed her underwear unless it wore out. When her son got sick, Hetty dressed like a poor person so she could get him treated at a charity hospital. The doctors and nurses saw through the disguise and refused to treat him. So, what does the wealthiest mom in the world do? She tried to treat him herself. Unfortunately, he had contracted gangrene. So in the end he had to have his leg amputated. Thanks, Mom. According to her "World's Greatest Miser" entry in the *Guinness Book of World Records*, Hetty Green died of apoplexy after arguing with a maid over the virtues of skimmed milk. Sounds about right.

WILLIAM ARCHIBALD SPOONER

William Archibald Spooner gave his name to that fun, linguistic turn of the tongue known as "spoonerism." It wasn't quite as much fun for old Billy, who was a professor at Oxford and who became so famous for his spooner-isms that people attended his lectures just to hear him make a mistake. Among my favor-ites—"Let us glaze our asses to the queer old Dean" (. . . raise our glasses to the dear old Queen).

SIMEON ELLERTON

Simeon Ellerton loved to walk long distances. His neighbors would often take advantage of this and ask him to run errands or make deliveries for them. For his own purposes, Simeon began to gather up stones from the roadside and carry them on his head. He carried enough to build himself a tidy little cottage. The only problem was that he had become so accustomed to walking with rocks on his head that he was uncomfortable without the added weight. His solution—and boy, was it simple—he just walked around with a bag of stones on his head for the rest of his life.

JOHN CHRISTIE

John Christie is a famed Brit-ish eccentric. Once while sit-ting next to the Queen during an opera, he removed his glass eye, cleaned it, put it back in its socket, and asked her if it was in straight! (He had an eye for all the pretty girls.) When he got too hot, he cut the arms off his formal jacket. He owned 180 handkerchiefs, 110 shirts, and despite paying tens of thousands of pounds to produce an opera, he traveled third class and carried his own luggage to avoid tipping. (I can see that.)

WILLIAM BUCKLAND

William Buckland filled his house with all types of animals and then proceeded to eat them (and serve them to guests). Various dinner guests described being served panther, crocodile, and mouse. Augustus Hare, a famous storyteller at the time, told this tale of Buckland: "Talk of strange relics led to mention of the heart of a French King [in fact, Louis XIV] preserved at Nuneham in a silver casket. Dr. Buckland, whilst looking at it, exclaimed, 'I have eaten many strange things, but have never eaten the heart of a king before,' and, before anyone could hinder him, he had gobbled it up, and the precious relic was lost forever." I suspect the phrase, "I'm so hungry I could eat a horse," was dreaded by all his kitchen staff.

CONCLUSION

"Schadenfreude ist die schönste Freude (denn sie kommt von Herzen)."

"Schadenfreude is the most beautiful kind of joy (since it comes directly from the heart)."

—Proverb

W hat a long, strange trip it's been. Writing this book, I was faced with the undeniable conclusion that there is a sameness that infects those giants of Schadenfreude. Whether they be pedophiles, rapists, egomaniacs, criminals, politicians, saints or sinners, they travel through life with blinders so tightly focused it's a wonder they don't end up with one eye. They blunder about the china shop of life making the bull look graceful. And we are mesmerized. Reality shows, 24-hour news networks, blogs ad nauseum—we can't take our eyes away from them. Half relieved it's not us and half waiting for them to slip on the banana peel, it's the obsession of the generation. Schadenfreude is not new; through the ages people have always found pleasure in the pain of others. I'm sure the earliest caveman learned to smile as he watched his companion become the morning snack for some saber-toothed lion. But we have taken it to new heights, and there is joy to be found.

INDEX

Nixon, Richard 6, 94, 98, 99,
100-103
Noguchi, Isamu 80
Nolin, Gena Lee 65
Non-Combatant 14
Normand, Mabel 40
Notting Hill 46
Nurse Nancy 53
NYPD Blue 60, 64

O'Malley, Austin 20
Obama, Barack 97, 104
O'Brien, Conan 59-60
Ocean's Eleven 70
Octavia 109
Octavian 109
O'Keeffe, Georgia 78
Ol' Blue Eyes 70
On Her Majesty's Secret Service
52
Onassis, Jackie Kennedy 112
Ono, Yoko 71
Oval Office 32
Ovitz, Michael 43-44
Oxford 76, 88, 136

Packwood, Robert 105
Palance, Jack 49-50
Pancho Villa 14
Papa Doc 97-98

Paramount 48
Paris 11
Patent Office 13
Paterson, David 96
Patton, George 16-17
Paul of Tarsus 7-8
Paul, Rand 100
Pavy, Benjamin 90
PBS 75
Peewee Herman 52-53
Peggy Shippen 10
Persians 17
Pesci, Joe 50
Peter III 110
Pfeiffer, Desmond 63
Philadelphia 10
Phillips Academy 130
Picasso, Pablo 78, 82
Playboy 31
Poe, Edgar Allen 73
Polanski, Roman 54
Pookie the Lion 58
Post Office 13
Powell, Lewis 12
Presley, Elvis 67, 80
Presley, Lisa Marie 45
Pretty Boy Floyd 90
Price-Waterhouse 50
Prime Minister of Great
Britain 14, 18

Westchester Premiere Theater 32
Western Union 13
Whedon, Joss 61
Wheeler, Adam 129-130
Whistler, James Abbott
   Mcneill 82
White Fang 58
White House 12, 32, 101
White, Snow 47
*Whole Lotta Shakin' Going
   On* 56
Wild Turkey 22
Wilde, Oscar 76
Will Mastin Trio 70
William Morris Agency 43
Williams, Robin 46
WNEW-TV 57
Wolf, Dick 63
Wonder Woman 61
Woods, Tiger 125

Woodward, Bob 99, 103
Woolworth Building 91
Working 55
World Church of the Cre-
   ator 25
World War I 22
WrestleMania 97
Wyler, William 50

Yearwood, Trisha 68
Yosemite Sam 41
Younger, Bob 119
Younger, Jim 119

Zell-Ravenheart, Oberon
   25-26
Zemeckis, Bob 51
Zima 133
Zima Clearmalt 133
Zimbalist Jr., Efrem 90

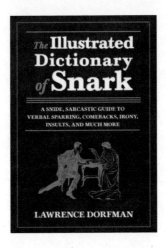

The Illustrated Dictionary of Snark
A Snide, Sarcastic Guide to Verbal Sparring, Comebacks, Irony, Insults, and Much More
by Lawrence Dorfman

What do Dorothy Parker, Groucho Marx, H. L. Mencken, Oscar Wilde, Robert Benchley, George Bernard Shaw, Jules Feiffer, Bill Hicks, Bill Maher, Phyllis Diller, Édith Piaf, W. C. Fields, Mark Twain, Voltaire, Charles Bukowski, and countless others have in common? Not a thing, other than each was a brilliantly snarky wit and all are included in this compendium of the original snark handbooks.

A minor literary success (beloved by both minors and miners), the snark handbooks have cemented their position in the literary world, high atop toilet seats everywhere. Now in one great big edition, this lofty tome promises to fulfill the need to chuckle, guffaw, titter, groan, and belly laugh as readers dip in and out of the great minds in literature, comedy, movies, music, and more. Proceed with caution.

$19.95 Hardcover • ISBN 978-1-62087-187-4

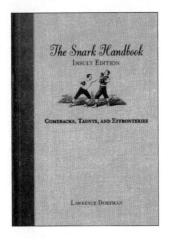

The Snark Handbook: Insult Edition
Comebacks, Taunts, and Effronteries
by Lawrence Dorfman

Author Lawrence Dorfman claims: "I love it when someone insults me. That means that I don't have to be nice anymore." In this latest incarnation of his bestselling series, Dorfman is in delicious form, dishing it out without any real consequences. The sharp-witted buyer (and that's you, my friend) may be wondering right about now: "Hey, how is this book any different from the first? That was full of insults, too." Yes, but these insults are different, and the author's retorts and taunts are so much more vitriolic than in the previous book.

Readers will find more material to actually use in day-to-day life, including streamlined instructions on when and how to mock your peers; how to use retorts with your spouse and children; and how our late, great ancestors used insults throughout history. This is not a mere collection of quotations. Dorfman speaks directly to his audience, serving as teacher, ringleader, and historian. After all, not all insults are snarky, and not all snark is insulting.

$12.95 Paperback • ISBN 978-1-61608-059-4

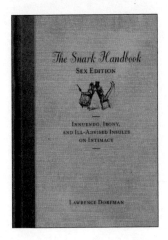

ALSO AVAILABLE

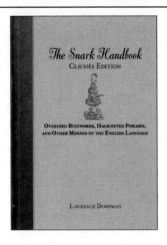

The Snark Handbook: Clichés Edition
Overused Buzzwords, Hackneyed Phrases, and Other Misuses of the English Language

by Lawrence Dorfman

In the words of Stephen Fry, "It is a cliché that most clichés are true, but then like most clichés, that cliché is untrue." Clichés are like rationalizations: try going a week without using one. It can't be done! They are the hobgoblin of little minds. For most of us, once you begin to take notice, they are fingernails on a chalkboard.

From Shakespeare to Shakira; in music, on television, at the movies; in the boardroom, on a conference call, online or in person, clichés have taken over the world. While some nitwits might say they're just misunderstood, they didn't start out that way. There was a time when they were new and vibrant, clever and pithy. Now they're just predictable—a vapid collection of much-too-familiar descriptions or metaphors that often replace smart conversation, speech, or writing.

This book is a collection of the most overused phrases of all time. Hopefully, it'll make you laugh. Hopefully, it'll make them think. And at the end of the day, if the early bird catches the worm and the slow and steady win the race . . . Please . . . kill . . . me . . . now.

$12.95 Paperback • ISBN 978-1-61608-635-0